FUNdamental Soccer

Written by **Karl Dewazien**
Coaching Director, California Youth Soccer Assn. -N.

I will use "HE", in this book, generically to refer to both boys and girls for the sake of brevity.

Karl Dewazien

FUN Soccer Enterprises
2904 Fine Ave.
Clovis, CA. 93612

I

Printed in the United States of America

Book design and Illustrations: **Joseph G. Garcia**

Editors: **Vincent J. Lavery**
Alan E. Maher

TABLE OF CONTENTS

IN MEMORY
DENNIS OLSON
He lived for Soccer

GENERAL TACTICS DEPENDS ON BALL POSSESSION

OUR BALL

Maintain ball possession

Go to goal and score

LOOSE BALL

Win ball

Go to goal and score

THEIR BALL

Regain ball possession

Prevent goals

THINK ABOUT IT!!!

FIRST STEPS FOR YOUNG PLAYERS
IN CONSIDERING TACTICS:

1. If our **team gains possession** of the ball, **all** our players are now **ATTACKERS**.

What are we now going to do to gain more ground to position ourselves to shoot and score?

WITH GOOD ATTACKING TACTICS YOU ARE MORE LIKELY TO SCORE ON YOUR OPPONENT.

2. If our **team loses possession** of the ball, **all** our players are now **DEFENDERS**.

What are we now going to do to prevent opponent from gaining advantageous positions and scoring?

WITH GOOD DEFENSIVE TACTICS YOU ARE MORE LIKELY TO PREVENT THE OPPONENT FROM SCORING.

3. It can be said that victory goes to the team which gains possession of the LOOSE ball. Therefore, a good practice should emphasize techniques which train players to be both mentally and physically ready to beat the opponent to ALL LOOSE balls.

What are we now going to do to win the battles for the loose ball?

WITH A PLAN FOR WINNING THE BATTLE TO LOOSE BALLS YOU ARE MORE LIKELY TO WIN THE GAME.

Prior Planning and Organized Practice Prevents Poor Game Performance.

The coach should be capable of observing his teams areas of strengths and weaknesses and to teach those tactics his team is able to carry-out. Prepare for the following:

> –*Strengths and weaknesses of players*
> –*Strengths and weaknesses of opponents*
> –*Players' understanding of the zones on the field*
> –*Players' understanding of channeling*
> –*Players' understanding of systems of play*
> –*Players' understanding of rules of the game*
> –*Travel arrangements*
> –*Ground conditions, weather, field size, etc....*

The skill level of tactics should advance in relation to the level of individual and team techniques. It is ridiculous for example to expect:

-accurate passes over long distances — when they can not pass accurately over the shorter distances.

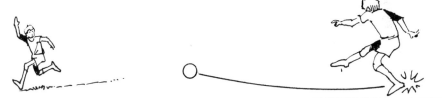

-precise passing through the air — when they can not pass accurately on the ground.

-good passing against an opponent — when they can not pass accurately in practice.

The team that does not work on tactics will inevitably play boot ball and run around the field in "herd" fashion.

HOW TO TEACH TACTICS:

OBSERVE: Other teams in action.

CHALK TALK—utilize chalk board, magnetic boards, butcher paper, etc., to visually show the player his role in each tactic being discussed.

FOLLOW UP—Sit down with each individual and explain his role in the team tactic being discussed.
- —Encourage the player to ask questions.
- —Check to see if he understands what you have just explained to him.
- —Ask him to tell you how he perceives his role.

This type of follow up should take place several times during the season.

4

EXPLANATION/DEMONSTRATION:

Step 1. **FUNdamental Stage**—No pressure—very slow pace (possible walking through sequence).

Step 2. **Game Related Stage**—Internal pressure.
Increased pace against the clock.
Increased pace against a stationary opponent.

Step 3. **Game Condition Stage**—Game pressure. Pace is dictated by the pressure of an actual opponent.

SMALL SIDED GAME:

Starting with a 1 vs. 1 game and increasing the number of teammates and opponents accordingly.

PRACTICE GAME:

Game played with the understanding that stops will occur to teach.

LEAGUE GAME:

The test to see if players have learned to apply principles which have been taught.

For more detailed instructions on teaching: Read — FUNdamental Soccer-Practice by Karl Dewazien, Fred Feathers Publishing Co. © 1985

FEEDBACK

HOW TO GET **FEEDBACK** FROM YOUR PLAYERS SO THAT YOU KNOW THEY UNDERSTAND YOUR DIRECTIONS AND CAN PUT THEM INTO PRACTICE.

1. Verbal quiz.
Have the players explain their areas of responsibiluty.

2. Reverse chalk talk.
Using a field of play, have the players draw out their positions, responsibilities, etc. . . . In other words, have a reverse chalk talk with the player teaching you and his teammates.

3. Written exam. (Highly recommended)
Give a written exam on rules, terminology and tactics that you think they should have mastered. The written test will quickly tell you the players understanding and maturity level, also what you can expect from them during the game.

To repeat—
This exam should be in writing.

SIMPLIFY THE TEACHING of TACTICS
by
DIVIDING THE FIELD INTO THREE ZONES...

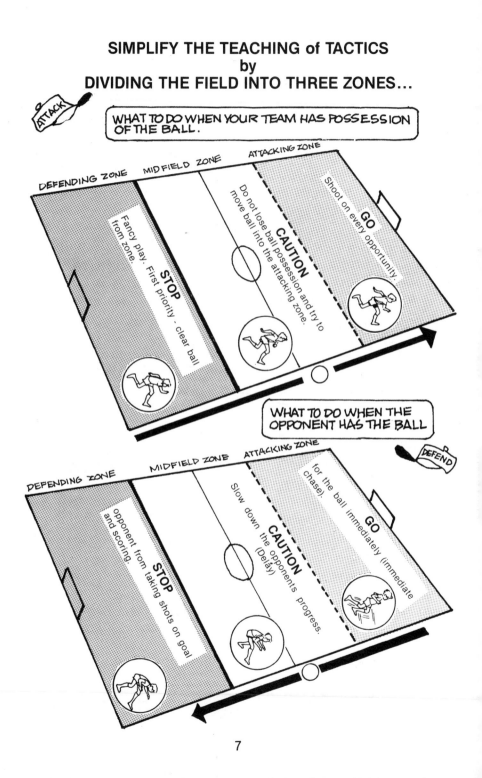

ATTACK

WHAT TO DO WHEN YOUR TEAM HAS POSSESSION OF THE BALL.

DEFENDING ZONE   MIDFIELD ZONE   ATTACKING ZONE

STOP
Fancy play. First priority - clear ball from zone.

CAUTION
Do not lose ball possession and try to move ball into the attacking zone.

GO
Shoot on every opportunity.

WHAT TO DO WHEN THE OPPONENT HAS THE BALL

DEFEND

DEFENDING ZONE   MIDFIELD ZONE   ATTACKING ZONE

STOP
opponent from taking shots on goal and scoring

CAUTION
Slow down the opponents progress.
(Delay)

GO
for the ball immediately (immediate chase).

SIMPLIFY THE TEACHING of TACTICS
by
DIVIDING THE FIELD INTO CHANNELS

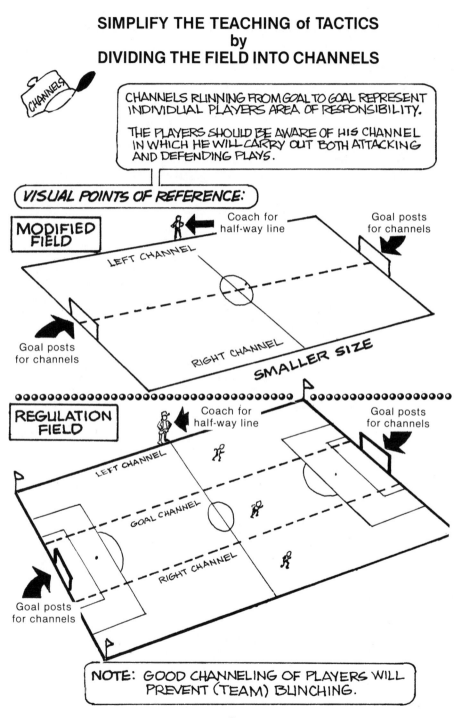

CHANNELS RUNNING FROM GOAL TO GOAL REPRESENT INDIVIDUAL PLAYERS AREA OF RESPONSIBILITY.

THE PLAYERS SHOULD BE AWARE OF HIS CHANNEL IN WHICH HE WILL CARRY OUT BOTH ATTACKING AND DEFENDING PLAYS.

VISUAL POINTS OF REFERENCE:

MODIFIED FIELD

Coach for half-way line

Goal posts for channels

LEFT CHANNEL

Goal posts for channels

RIGHT CHANNEL

SMALLER SIZE

REGULATION FIELD

Coach for half-way line

Goal posts for channels

LEFT CHANNEL

GOAL CHANNEL

RIGHT CHANNEL

Goal posts for channels

NOTE: GOOD CHANNELING OF PLAYERS WILL PREVENT (TEAM) BUNCHING.

IN ADDITION TO VISUAL AIDS, COACHES MAY CHOOSE TO USE WRIST BANDS OR HEAD BANDS OF DIFFERENT COLORS TO INDICATE AREA OF RESPONSIBILITY.

Examples:

Players in left channel:
Wear sweat band on left wrist.

Players in goal channel:
Wear sweat band on each wrist.
Wear no sweat bands.
OR — Wear a head band.

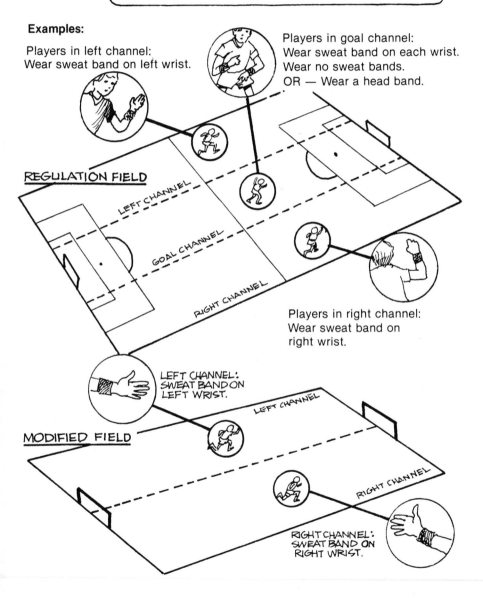

REGULATION FIELD

LEFT CHANNEL

GOAL CHANNEL

RIGHT CHANNEL

Players in right channel:
Wear sweat band on right wrist.

LEFT CHANNEL:
SWEAT BAND ON
LEFT WRIST.

MODIFIED FIELD

LEFT CHANNEL

RIGHT CHANNEL

RIGHT CHANNEL:
SWEAT BAND ON
RIGHT WRIST.

WHEN THE BALL IS IN THE FURTHEST CHANNEL, PLAYERS SHOULD MOVE ACROSS TO THE EDGE OF THEIR CHANNEL TO COVER / SUPPORT THEIR TEAMMATES.

HOWEVER, THEY SHOULD AVOID RUNNING PAST THEIR TEAMMATES IN THE GOAL CHANNEL SINCE THIS WOULD LEAD TO "**BUNCHING-UP**" AND LEAVE TOO MUCH OF THE FIELD UNATTENDED.

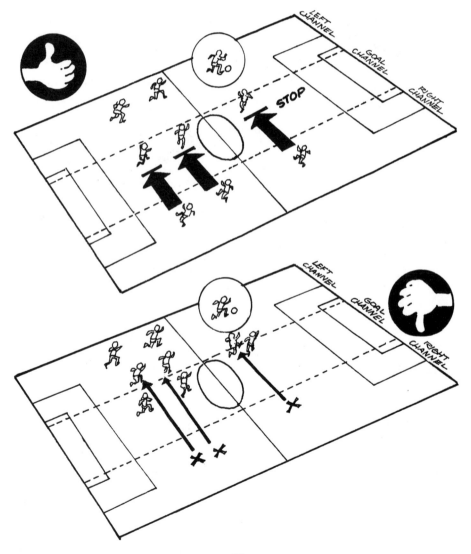

PLAYERS POSITIONS

THE RESPONSIBILITIES OF THE PLAYERS HAVE TRADITIONALLY BEEN DIVIDED INTO *THREE LINES*

| Ⓑ Backs | Ⓜ Midfielders | Ⓕ Forwards |

Depending on ball possession duties on each line change.

IF YOUR TEAM HAS BALL POSSESSION the three lines may be termed:

Ⓑ Attacking Backs Ⓜ Attacking Midfielders Ⓕ Attacking Forwards

IF OPPONENT HAS BALL POSSESSION the three lines may be termed:

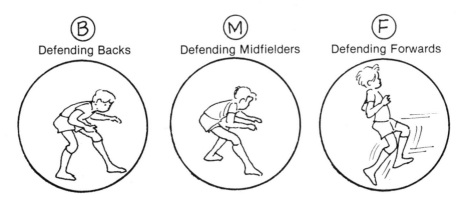

Ⓑ Defending Backs Ⓜ Defending Midfielders Ⓕ Defending Forwards

NOTE: On any loose ball player nearest ball becomes the primary attack player.

Players must be taught to play both offensively and defensively.

11

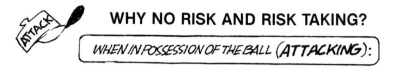

WHY NO RISK AND RISK TAKING?

WHEN IN POSSESSION OF THE BALL **(ATTACKING):**

BACKS – Should remember they only have the **Goalkeeper behind them for support** with Midfielders and Forwards in front of them.

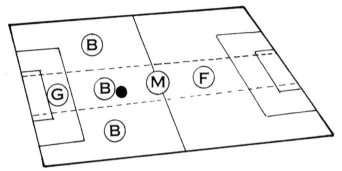

MIDFIELDERS — Should remember they have a Backs behind them and Forwards in front of them for support.

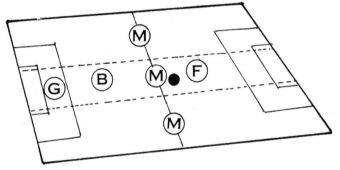

FORWARDS — Should remember they have no one in front of them and Midfielders and Backs behind them for support.

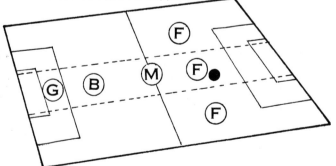

Note: Be able to distinguish when to take a chance on both attack and defense according to your position on the field.

WHEN OPPONENT HAS POSSESSION OF THE BALL (**DEFENDING**)

FORWARDS — Should remember they have Midfielders and Backs behind them for defensive cover.

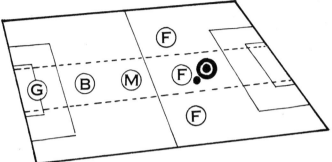

MIDFIELDERS — Should remember they have Backs behind them for cover and Forwards in front of them.

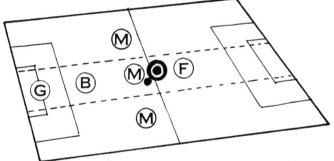

BACKS — Should remember they only have Goalkeeper behind them for cover with Midfielders and Forwards in front of them.

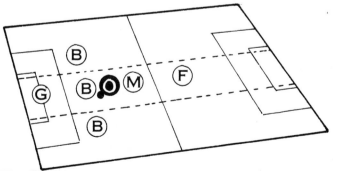

Note: Be able to distinguish when to take a chance on both attack and defense according to your position on the field.

13

EXCHANGING POSITIONS

THE PLAYERS MUST UNDERSTAND THAT THEY ARE *"FREE"* TO PLAY ON ANY PART OF THE FIELD

PLAYERS SHOULD BE ENCOURAGED TO EXCHANGE POSITIONS PROVIDING THEY WORK TO SUPPORT AND COVER FOR EACH OTHER.

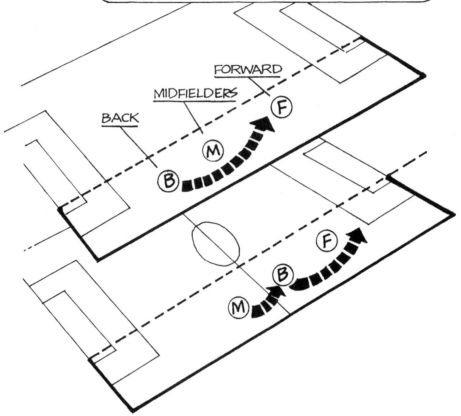

RECOMMENDATIONS:
—Younger players in the beginning should exchange positions inside their channel. Moving vertically — that is from goal to goal.

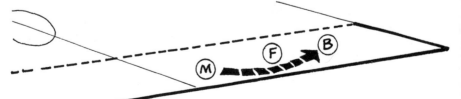

NOTE: Exchanging permits a player from one line to move into another line so that his defense or attack is not weakened as a result.

14

FORMATION or SYSTEM of PLAY

MODIFIED & SYSTEMS

> SYSTEM IS THE SENSIBLE DISTRIBUTION OF THE PLAYERS TO COVER THE LENGTH AND WIDTH OF THE FIELD. *for example:*

Under 8 = 2-2-2

Under 10 = 3-3-2

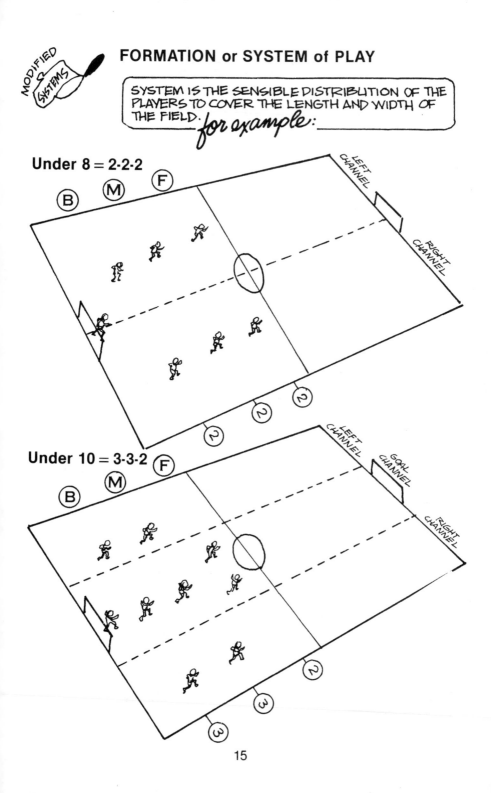

Under 12 = 3-3-3 Putting eleventh player on the field where needed according to the strengths and weaknesses of the opponent.

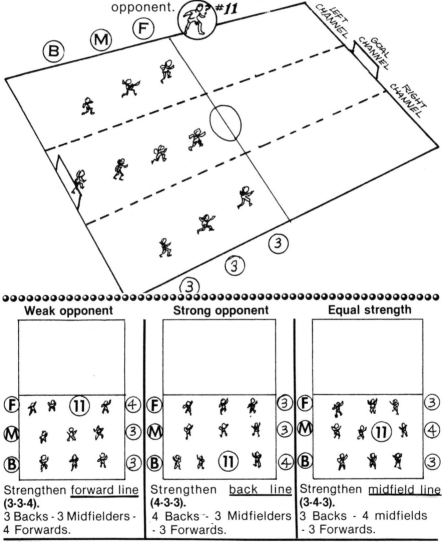

Weak opponent	Strong opponent	Equal strength
Strengthen <u>forward line</u> (3-3-4).	Strengthen <u>back line</u> (4-3-3).	Strengthen <u>midfield line</u> (3-4-3).
3 Backs - 3 Midfielders - 4 Forwards.	4 Backs - 3 Midfielders - 3 Forwards.	3 Backs - 4 midfields - 3 Forwards.

NOTE:
Do not fit your players into a system, rather make the system fit your players.

Some Thoughts on Systems of Play

FACTS

THE SKILL LEVEL OF THE OPPONENT, FIELD CONDITIONS, WEATHER CONDITIONS ETC... WILL SUGGEST THE SYSTEM YOU SHOULD USE.

for example:

- If the opponent is stronger you will strengthen your back line.
- If you are stronger you will strengthen the front line.
- If the teams are of equal strength—it is best to strengthen the midfield line.
- If the field is wet you may use high passing and start those players who can kick and control the <u>high ball</u>.

- As the players mature and realize that the ball never gets tired they will teach themselves to restrict their running habits.
- Teach the FUNdamentals of technique and tactics will begin to take shape.
- Without basic skills players will have difficulty in carrying out any tactical assignment.

SYSTEMS (continued)

THE IDEAL TEAM IS THE TEAM WHERE EACH PLAYER CAN PLAY ANY POSITION AND PLAY IT WELL. HOWEVER, DO NOT COUNT ON SUCH LUXURY.

Therefore,

— Look at the individual's strengths and weaknesses.
— Look at the individual's ability to dribble, pass and shoot.
— Let the players feel comfortable in their assigned duties.
— Explain the system in advance of the game and what is expected of each player.
— Do not play a player in an unfamiliar position.

Use stronger players in goal channel.
Use weaker players in outer channels.
Use taller players in the back line.
Faster players in the front line.
"One-hundred per centers" in the midfield line.

What is the most successful SYSTEM?
IF IT WORKS IT IS RIGHT!

THE PLAIN FACTS:

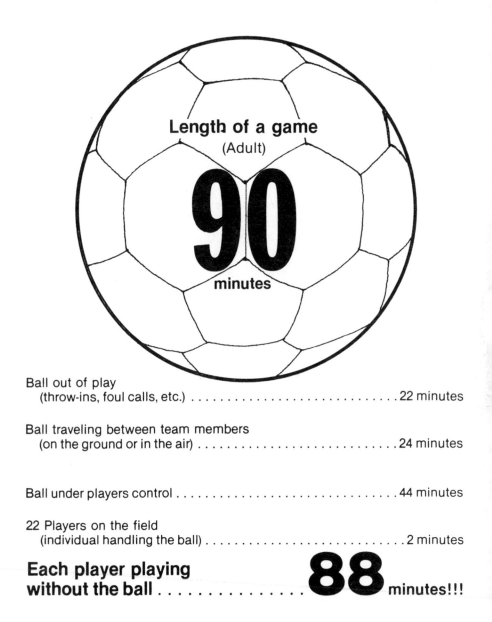

Length of a game
(Adult)

90

minutes

Ball out of play
(throw-ins, foul calls, etc.) . . . . .22 minutes

Ball traveling between team members
(on the ground or in the air) . . . . .24 minutes

Ball under players control . . . . .44 minutes

22 Players on the field
(individual handling the ball) . . . . .2 minutes

**Each player playing
without the ball** . . . . **88** minutes!!!

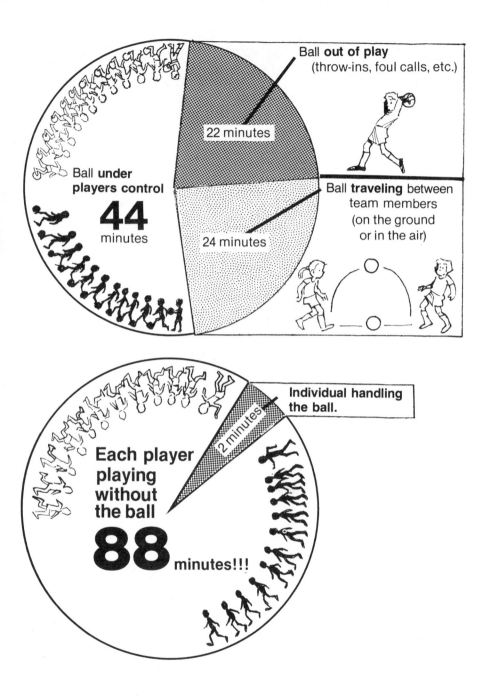

Ball **out of play**
(throw-ins, foul calls, etc.)

22 minutes

Ball **under**
players control
44
minutes

24 minutes

Ball **traveling** between
team members
(on the ground
or in the air)

Individual handling
the ball.

2 minutes

Each player
playing
without
the ball
88minutes!!!

THINK ABOUT IT!

20

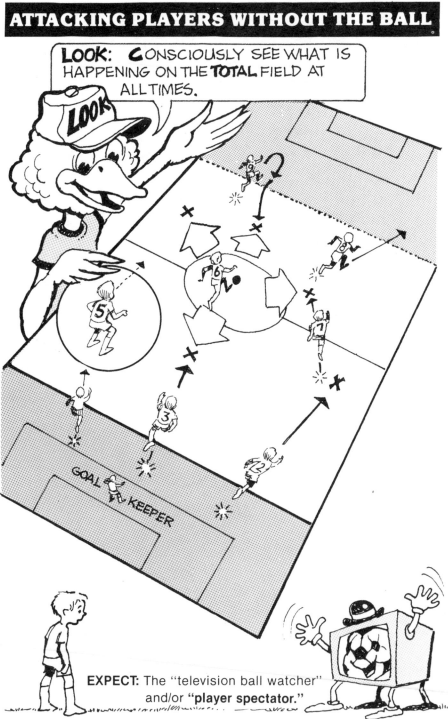

ATTACKING PLAYERS WITHOUT THE BALL

IN OTHER WORDS **SEE** THE PRESENT SITUATION AND ANTICIPATE
YOUR FUTURE OPTIONS.

ATTACKING PLAYERS WITHOUT THE BALL

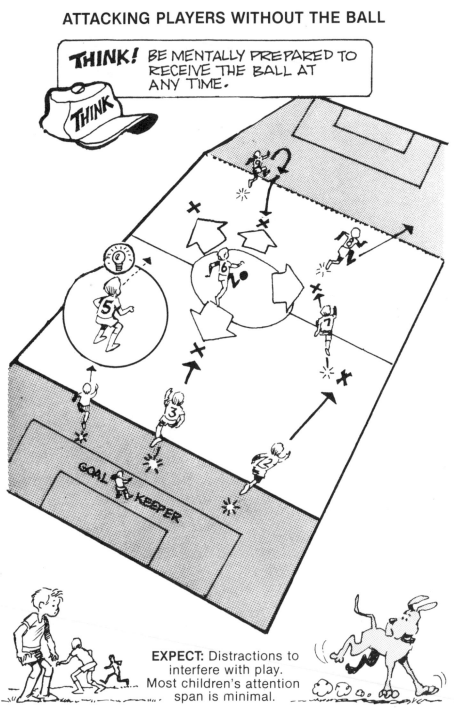

THINK! BE MENTALLY PREPARED TO RECEIVE THE BALL AT ANY TIME.

EXPECT: Distractions to interfere with play. Most children's attention span is minimal.

ATTACKING PLAYERS WITHOUT THE BALL

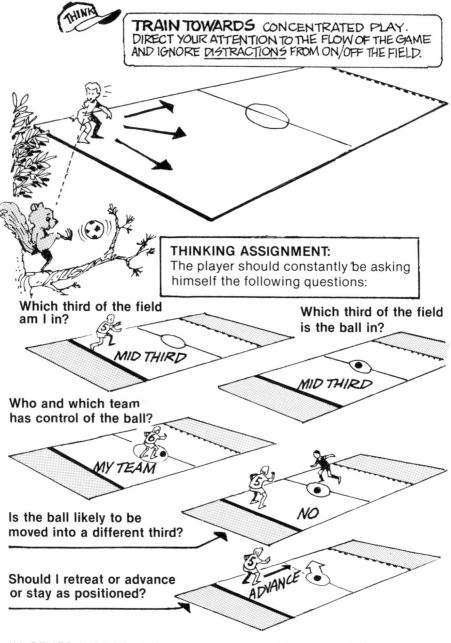

TRAIN TOWARDS CONCENTRATED PLAY.
DIRECT YOUR ATTENTION TO THE FLOW OF THE GAME
AND IGNORE DISTRACTIONS FROM ON/OFF THE FIELD.

THINKING ASSIGNMENT:
The player should constantly be asking
himself the following questions:

Which third of the field am I in?

MID THIRD

Which third of the field is the ball in?

MID THIRD

Who and which team has control of the ball?

MY TEAM

NO

Is the ball likely to be moved into a different third?

Should I retreat or advance or stay as positioned?

ADVANCE

IN OTHER WORDS **READ** THE PRESENT SITUATION AND
ANTICIPATE YOUR FUTURE MOVEMENT(S).

ATTACKING PLAYERS WITHOUT THE BALL

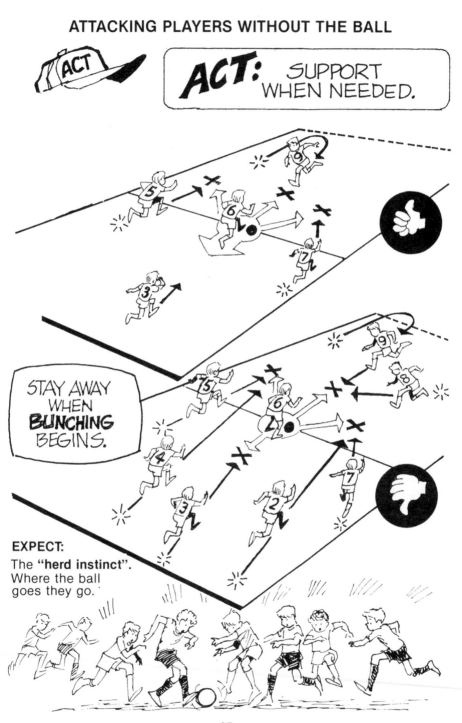

ACT: SUPPORT WHEN NEEDED.

STAY AWAY WHEN **BUNCHING** BEGINS.

EXPECT:

The **"herd instinct"**.
Where the ball
goes they go.

ATTACKING PLAYERS WITHOUT THE BALL

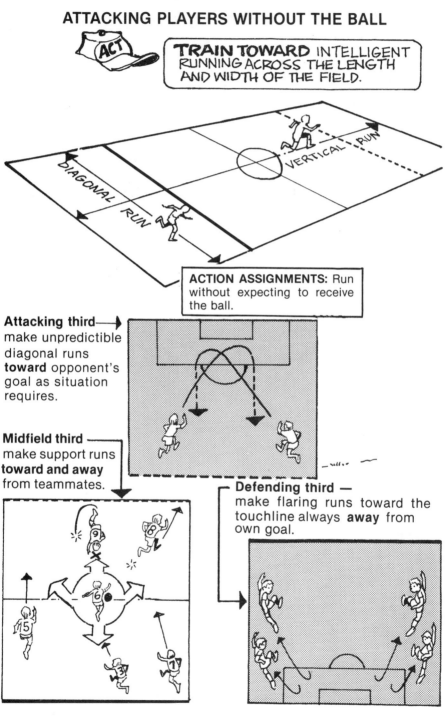

TRAIN TOWARD INTELLIGENT RUNNING ACROSS THE LENGTH AND WIDTH OF THE FIELD.

DIAGONAL RUN

VERTICAL RUN

ACTION ASSIGNMENTS: Run without expecting to receive the ball.

Attacking third—➤
make unpredictible diagonal runs **toward** opponent's goal as situation requires.

Midfield third ——
make support runs **toward and away** from teammates.

Defending third —
make flaring runs toward the touchline always **away** from own goal.

SUPPORT RUN – GET INTO A POSITION FOR A PASS.

RUNNING OFF THE BALL. GET RID OF OPPONENT FOR A PASS.

DUMMY RUN – TAKE OPPONENT OUT OF GOOD DEFENDING POSITION.

MOVE

ATTACKING PLAYERS WITHOUT THE BALL

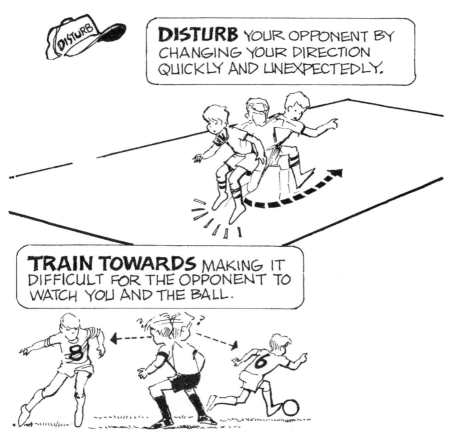

DISTURB YOUR OPPONENT BY CHANGING YOUR DIRECTION QUICKLY AND UNEXPECTEDLY.

TRAIN TOWARDS MAKING IT DIFFICULT FOR THE OPPONENT TO WATCH YOU AND THE BALL.

PLAYERS ASSIGNMENT:

Move to confuse the opponent — For example: Backward, laterally, slow, fast or with sudden stops according to the needs of the moment.

PACING: LEARN TO CONSERVE YOUR ENERGY.

PUFF! PUFF!

PLENTY OF HEART BUT TO NO AVAIL.

TRAIN TOWARDS: WALKING WHEN I'TS TIME TO WALK, JOG WHEN IT'S TIME TO JOG, RUN WHEN IT'S TIME TO RUN AND SPRINT WHEN IT'S TIME TO SPRINT.

WALK	JOG	RUN	SPRINT

PLAYERS ASSIGNMENT:
Adjust your movements/runs to the flow of the game and the positioning of the ball.

WHEN ONE LEARNS TO **READ** THE GAME PACING WILL FOLLOW AUTOMATICALLY.

GLANCE: CONSCIOUSLY SEE WHAT IS HAPPENING IN *YOUR IMMEDIATE AREA.* PUTTING YOURSELF IN A POSITION TO RECEIVE/CONTROL THE BALL WITH MINIMUM HINDERANCE.

TRAIN TOWARDS: LOOKING OVER BOTH LEFT AND RIGHT SHOULDERS WHILE APPROACHING THE BALL.

GLANCING ASSIGNMENT:

1 Where are the most threatening opponents?

2 Where are teammates who are in the best position(s) to assist you?

3 What options of play are available?

31

MOVING TO THE BALL

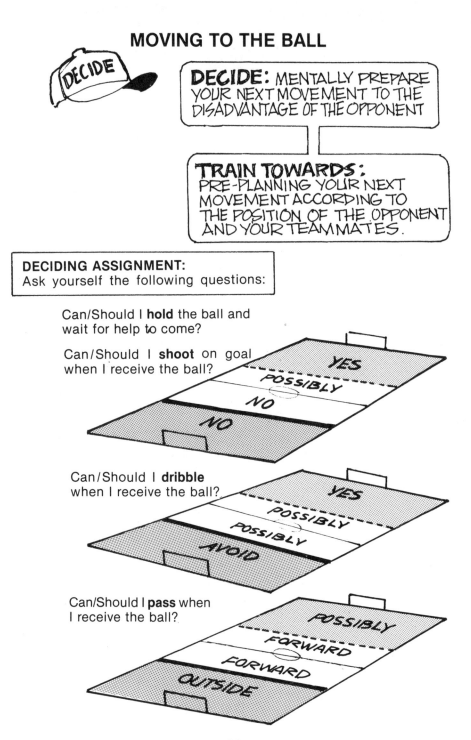

DECIDE: MENTALLY PREPARE YOUR NEXT MOVEMENT TO THE DISADVANTAGE OF THE OPPONENT

TRAIN TOWARDS: PRE-PLANNING YOUR NEXT MOVEMENT ACCORDING TO THE POSITION OF THE OPPONENT AND YOUR TEAMMATES.

DECIDING ASSIGNMENT:
Ask yourself the following questions:

Can/Should I **hold** the ball and wait for help to come?

Can/Should I **shoot** on goal when I receive the ball?

YES
POSSIBLY
NO
NO

Can/Should I **dribble** when I receive the ball?

YES
POSSIBLY
POSSIBLY
AVOID

Can/Should I **pass** when I receive the ball?

POSSIBLY
FORWARD
FORWARD
OUTSIDE

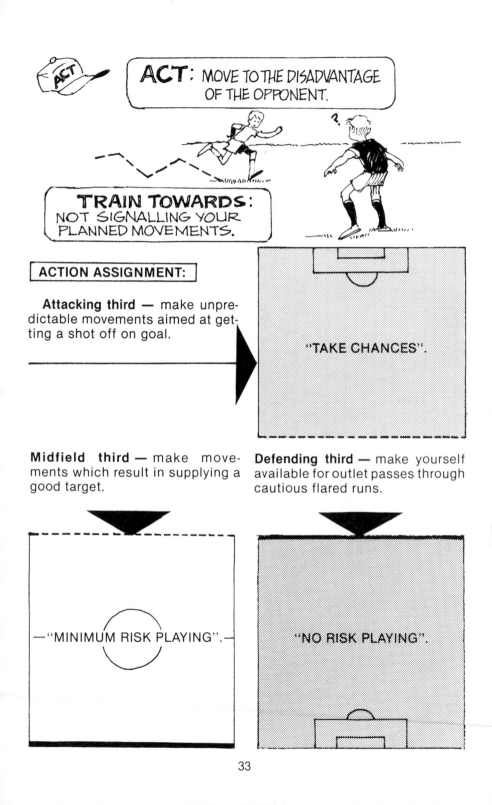

ACT: MOVE TO THE DISADVANTAGE OF THE OPPONENT.

TRAIN TOWARDS: NOT SIGNALLING YOUR PLANNED MOVEMENTS.

ACTION ASSIGNMENT:

Attacking third — make unpredictable movements aimed at getting a shot off on goal.

"TAKE CHANCES".

Midfield third — make movements which result in supplying a good target.

"MINIMUM RISK PLAYING".

Defending third — make yourself available for outlet passes through cautious flared runs.

"NO RISK PLAYING".

MOVING TO THE BALL

ALWAYS MOVE TO THE BALL:
STEP TOWARDS THE BALL. DO NOT
WAIT FOR THE BALL TO REACH YOU.

TRAIN TOWARDS:
APPROACHING EVERY BALL.

MOVING ASSIGNMENT:

**NEVER LET THE BALL REACH YOU —
YOU REACH IT FIRST.**

For quick control.
Beat the opponent to the ball.

MOVING TO THE BALL

PREPARE: MOVE TO THE BALL BY FIRST MOVING *AWAY*- TO TAKE OPPONENT IN THE WRONG DIRECTION.

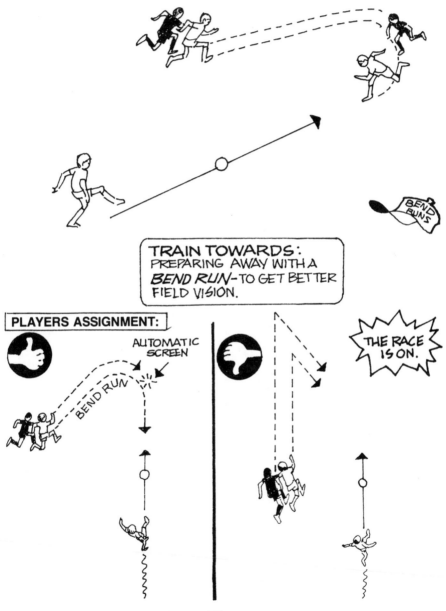

TRAIN TOWARDS: PREPARING AWAY WITH A *BEND RUN*- TO GET BETTER FIELD VISION.

PLAYERS ASSIGNMENT:

AUTOMATIC SCREEN

BEND RUN

THE RACE IS ON.

MOVING TO THE BALL

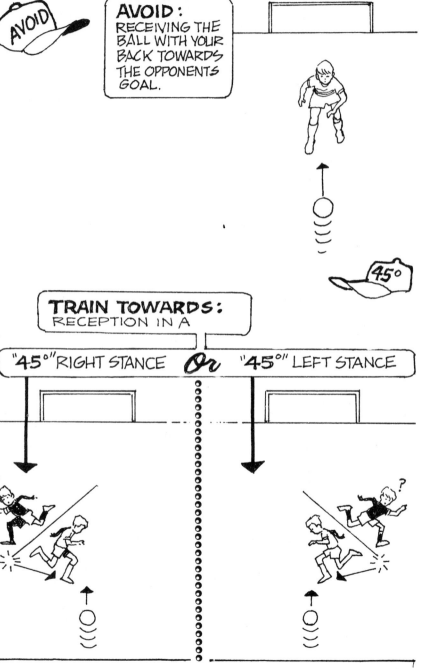

MOVING TO THE BALL

FAKE : Approach the ball with movements that confuse the opponent.

TRAIN TOWARDS: Additional skills which allow for faking or feinting.

(2.) "Jab step right move ball to the left".

(2.) "Jab step left move ball to the right".

JAB STEP: Fake/Feint in one direction with one sharp "plant" step or shoulder dip and take ball in the opposite direction.

37

MOVING TO THE BALL

TURN TOWARDS OPPONENTS GOAL WITH BALL WHEN PLAY PERMITS **OR** FOLLOW BALL IF THROUGH PASS HAS BEEN ALLOWED.

EXPECT THIS:
1. TURNING BALL INTO THE OPPONENT.
2. PLAY/MOVING BALL WITH FOOT CLOSEST TO OPPONENT.
3. PUSHING BALL TOO FAR AWAY SO POSSESSION IS LOST.

TRAIN TOWARDS THIS:
1. SCREENING THE BALL FROM OPPONENT BY KEEPING BODY BETWEEN BALL AND OPPONENT.
2. PLAY/MOVE BALL WITH FOOT AWAY FROM OPPONENT.

TURNING ASSIGNMENTS:
Controlled turn of body and ball — opposite of fake.

Opponent right – Jab Step right –
TURN LEFT:

Opponent left – Jab Step left –
TURN RIGHT:

MOVING TO THE BALL

ALLOW NO BALL TO STOP!

EXPECT THIS:
TOTAL STOPPAGE OF BALL, GIVING THE OPPONENT TIME TO ADJUST.

TRAIN TOWARDS THIS:
REDIRECTING THE BALL — IF FAKE IS USED MOVE BALL IN OPPOSITE DIRECTION.

Control and play the ball in one motion

PLAYERS ASSIGNMENT

Hold or Control the ball without totally stopping it.

39

MOVING TO THE BALL

PERFECTION ALLOWS FOR NO BALL TO BOUNCE. IF POSSIBLE WORK TOWARDS MEETING BALL BEFORE IT BOUNCES.

EXPECT THIS: SHYING AWAY FROM THE BALL.

TRAIN TOWARDS THIS: CONTROL AND PLAY.

Gain control of the ball before it bounces. Carry out your planned movement.

THE PLAIN FACTS.

HIS ONLY
OPTIONS ARE:

1. **SHOOT** the ball.

2. **DRIBBLE** the ball.   3. **PASS** the ball.

4. **SHIELD** the ball.

THINK ABOUT IT!

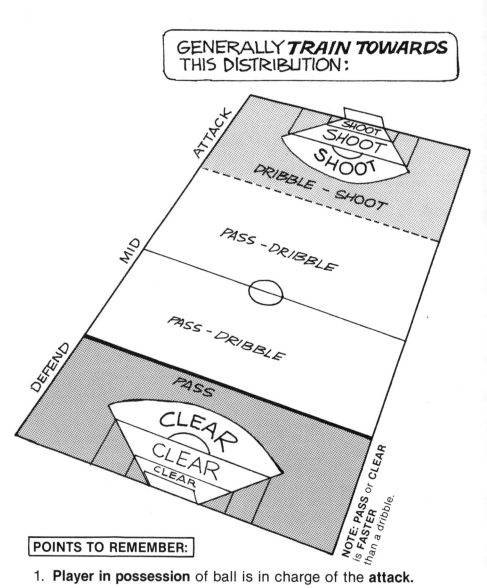

POINTS TO REMEMBER:

1. **Player in possession** of ball is in charge of the **attack.**

2. The **objective** of an attack is to **maintain ball possession.**

3. The **ultimate objective** of every attack is to **score.**

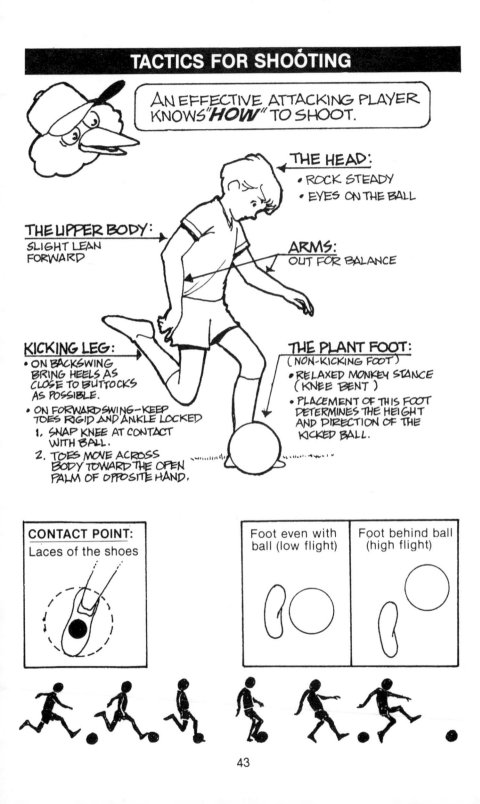

TACTICS FOR SHOOTING

AN EFFECTIVE ATTACKING PLAYER KNOWS *"HOW"* TO SHOOT.

THE HEAD:
- ROCK STEADY
- EYES ON THE BALL

THE UPPER BODY:
SLIGHT LEAN FORWARD

ARMS:
OUT FOR BALANCE

KICKING LEG:
- ON BACKSWING BRING HEELS AS CLOSE TO BUTTOCKS AS POSSIBLE.
- ON FORWARD SWING—KEEP TOES RIGID AND ANKLE LOCKED
  1. SNAP KNEE AT CONTACT WITH BALL.
  2. TOES MOVE ACROSS BODY TOWARD THE OPEN PALM OF OPPOSITE HAND.

THE PLANT FOOT:
(NON-KICKING FOOT)
- RELAXED MONKEY STANCE (KNEE BENT)
- PLACEMENT OF THIS FOOT DETERMINES THE HEIGHT AND DIRECTION OF THE KICKED BALL.

CONTACT POINT:
Laces of the shoes

Foot even with ball (low flight)

Foot behind ball (high flight)

TACTICS FOR SHOOTING

GLANCE: CONSCIOUSLY SEE WHAT IS HAPPENING IN YOUR IMMEDIATE AREA. PUT YOURSELF IN A POSITION TO SHOOT THE BALL WITH ACCURACY AND MINIMUM HINDERANCE FROM OPPONENT.

FACING THE GOAL:

BACK TO THE GOAL:
(45° STANCE)

TRAIN TOWARDS
TAKING A QUICK GLANCE TO SEE WHERE THE GOAL-KEEPER IS POSITIONED.

TRAIN TOWARDS
TAKING QUICK GLANCES BOTH TO THE RIGHT AND LEFT SIDE OF YOU.

GLANCING ASSIGNMENT:

Where is the goalkeeper positioned?
Where is the goalmouth (near and far post)?
Where is the nearest obstructing opponent?

POINT TO REMEMBER:

The ability to shoot at the right moment is directly related to the players glancing efficiency.

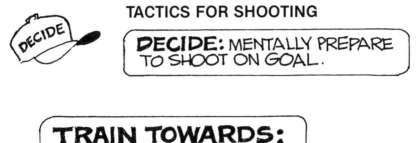

TACTICS FOR SHOOTING

DECIDE: MENTALLY PREPARE TO SHOOT ON GOAL.

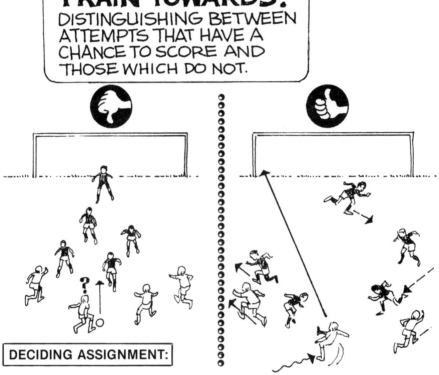

TRAIN TOWARDS: DISTINGUISHING BETWEEN ATTEMPTS THAT HAVE A CHANCE TO SCORE AND THOSE WHICH DO NOT.

DECIDING ASSIGNMENT:

In making the decision to shoot check the following:

1. Am I within my shooting range?

2. Can I shoot on goal when I receive the ball?

3. Will I have to shoot with left or right foot?

FACT: It takes approximately 10 shots on goal to score one goal in a game.

TACTICS FOR SHOOTING

ACT: SHOOT THE BALL IF THERE IS A CHANCE OF YOU SCORING. HOWEVER, REMEMBER TO PASS THE BALL IF TEAM-MATE IS IN BETTER POSITION TO SHOOT.

TRAIN TOWARDS: NOT HESITATING IN TAKING A SHOT WHEN INSIDE YOUR SHOOTING RANGE.

"It is better to have shot and missed than never to have taken a shot at all."

WHEN IN DOUBT --- SHOOT!!

FACT: One hundred per cent of all shots not taken--will never result in a goal.

46

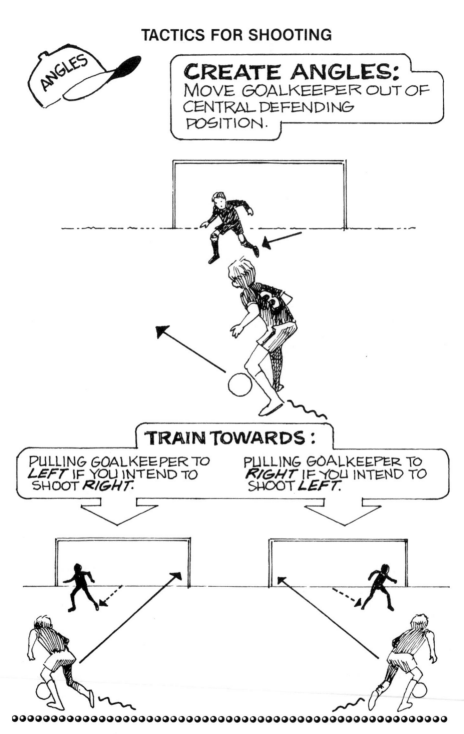

CREATE ANGLES: MOVE GOALKEEPER OUT OF CENTRAL DEFENDING POSITION.

TRAIN TOWARDS:

PULLING GOALKEEPER TO *LEFT* IF YOU INTEND TO SHOOT *RIGHT*.

PULLING GOALKEEPER TO *RIGHT* IF YOU INTEND TO SHOOT *LEFT*.

TACTICS FOR SHOOTING

SHOOT LOW.
WORLD CUP (1986) STATISTIC:
"EIGHTY PERCENT OF THE GOALS
WERE SCORED INTO THE LOWER
HALF OF THE NET (FOUR FEET OR
LESS FROM THE GROUND)."*

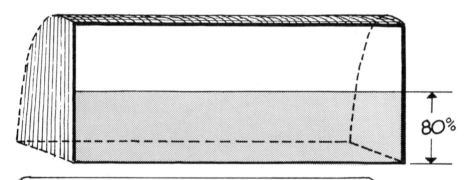

80%

TRAIN TOWARDS: KEEPING THE BALL
AS LOW IN FLIGHT AS POSSIBLE.

Contact the ball about mid-way
point or above.

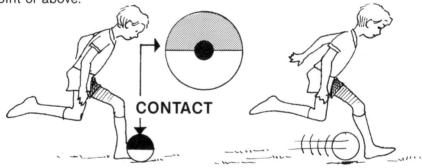

CONTACT

If rolling away place plant foot
in front of ball.

*Statistics recorded by Zvi Friedman and Zeev Zalster Wingate Institute for Physical Education and Sport.

TACTICS FOR SHOOTING

SHOOT TO NEAR AND FAR POSTS.
WORLD CUP (1986) STATISTIC:
"EIGHTY-SIX PERCENT OF ALL GOALS
WERE SCORED INTO THE LOWER
CORNERS OF THE NET."*

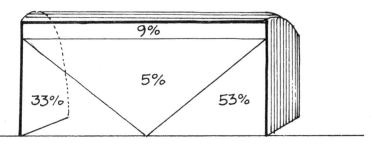

TRAIN TOWARDS: SCORING ON BOTH
SIDES OF THE GOALKEEPER AT THE NEAR
AND FAR POSTS.

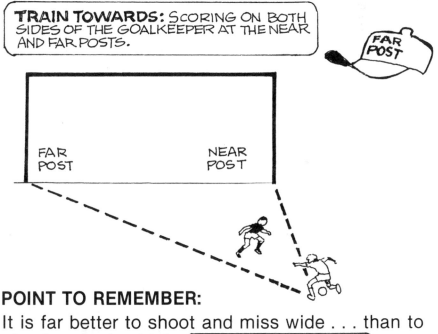

POINT TO REMEMBER:

It is far better to shoot and miss wide . . . than to
shoot and miss high. (THERE IS A CHANCE OF DEFLECTION)

*Statistics recorded by Zvi Friedman And Zeev Zalster Wingate Institute for Physical
Education and Sport.

TACTICS FOR SHOOTING

DECEPTION: DO NOT TELEGRAPH UPCOMING SHOT.

KEEP THE ELEMENT OF SURPRISE AS YOUR WEAPON AGAINST THE GOALKEEPER.

AVOID: EXAGERATED LEG ACTION WHICH TELLS KEEPER TO PREPARE FOR COMING SHOT AND TYPE OF SHOT YOU ARE ABOUT TO TAKE.

TRAIN TOWARDS: SHOOTING ON THE RUN WITHOUT BREAKING STRIDE.

IF POSSIBLE TAKE A FIRST TIME SHOT ON GOAL.

TACTICS FOR SHOOTING

FOLLOW YOUR SHOT. FOLLOW EACH AND EVERY SHOT MENTALLY AND PHYSICALLY.

AVOID: ADMIRING THE FLIGHT OF THE BALL UNTIL ITS CONCLUSION.

YOU CAN READ OF THE RESULTS IN THE PAPER NEXT MORNING!!

TRAIN TOWARDS: FOLLOWING EACH AND EVERY SHOT IMMEDIATELY TO RECOVER ANY REBOUND FROM POSTS, FIELD PLAYERS, GOALKEEPER OR REFEREE.

FAKE SHOT ON GOAL!

TRAIN TOWARDS: MAKING GOALKEEPER BELIEVE YOU ARE ABOUT TO SHOOT AND THEN TAKE ADVANTAGE OF HIS INITIAL MOVEMENT.

MAINTAIN THAT ELEMENT OF SURPRISE !!

CHOOSE ACCURACY OVER POWER. A SHOT ON TARGET HAS A CHANCE TO SCORE

AVOID: POWERFUL KICKS AT THE BALL WHICH CAN RESULT IN:

TOTALLY MISSING THE BALL.

TOTALLY MISSING THE GOAL.

TRAIN TOWARDS: INTELLIGENT PLACEMENT OF THE BALL.

TACTICS OF DRIBBLING

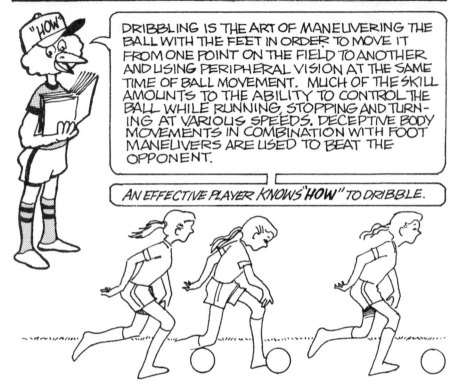

DRIBBLING IS THE ART OF MANEUVERING THE BALL WITH THE FEET IN ORDER TO MOVE IT FROM ONE POINT ON THE FIELD TO ANOTHER AND USING PERIPHERAL VISION AT THE SAME TIME OF BALL MOVEMENT. MUCH OF THE SKILL AMOUNTS TO THE ABILITY TO CONTROL THE BALL WHILE RUNNING, STOPPING AND TURNING AT VARIOUS SPEEDS. DECEPTIVE BODY MOVEMENTS IN COMBINATION WITH FOOT MANEUVERS ARE USED TO BEAT THE OPPONENT.

AN EFFECTIVE PLAYER KNOWS "**HOW**" TO DRIBBLE.

KEY POINTS:

1. The upper body should be tilted slightly forward — to further screen the ball.

2. The ball should be played (touched) on the side of the toe using either the inside or outside of the foot.

LEFT SHOE		RIGHT SHOE	
OUTSIDE INSTEP	INSIDE INSTEP	INSIDE INSTEP	OUTSIDE INSTEP

3. The eyes should be fixed partially on the ball — in addition to peripherally encompassing "the action around the player".

TACTICS OF DRIBBLING

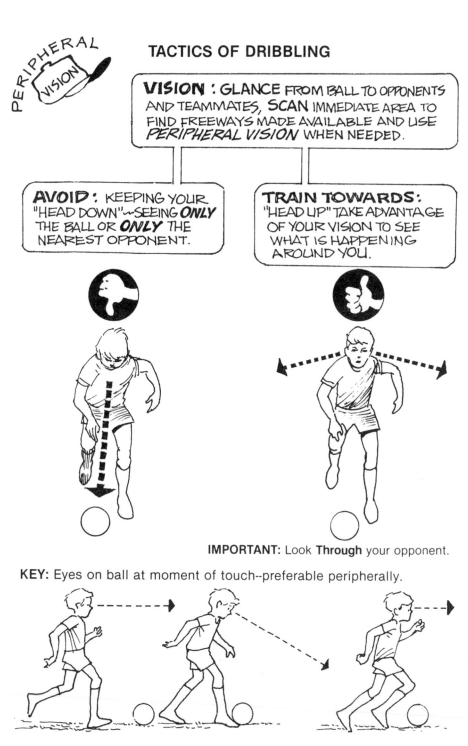

PERIPHERAL VISION

VISION : GLANCE FROM BALL TO OPPONENTS AND TEAMMATES, **SCAN** IMMEDIATE AREA TO FIND FREEWAYS MADE AVAILABLE AND USE *PERIPHERAL VISION* WHEN NEEDED.

AVOID : KEEPING YOUR "HEAD DOWN"~SEEING *ONLY* THE BALL OR *ONLY* THE NEAREST OPPONENT.

TRAIN TOWARDS: "HEAD UP" TAKE ADVANTAGE OF YOUR VISION TO SEE WHAT IS HAPPENING AROUND YOU.

IMPORTANT: Look **Through** your opponent.

KEY: Eyes on ball at moment of touch--preferable peripherally.

TACTICS OF DRIBBLING

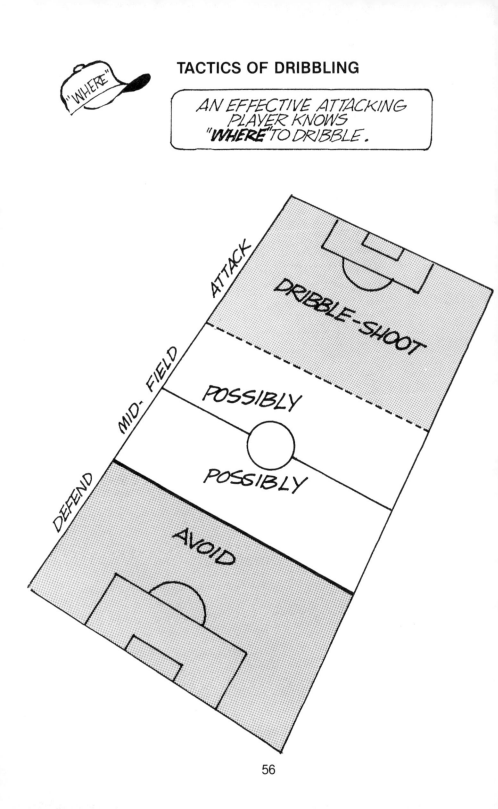

*AN EFFECTIVE ATTACKING PLAYER KNOWS "**WHERE**" TO DRIBBLE.*

TACTICS OF DRIBBLING

DECIDE : WHILE DRIBBLING MAKE A PERSONAL JUDGEMENT ON WHAT IS OR IS NOT AN APPROPRIATE COURSE OF ACTION.

MAKE THE ELEMENT OF SURPRISE A PRIMARY FACTOR

Consider some of the following situations when making your decision:

-Am I being challenged?

-Can I clear myself for a shot on goal?

-Are there any teammates in better positions to advance the ball?

-Can I entice the opponent out of good defending positions with my dribble thereby placing a teammate in a better position to shoot or advance the ball?

-Can I get past the opponent and gain numerical advantage as a result?

-Should I slow down and wait for support?

-Are we leading and how much time is left on the clock?

An effective player knows "when" and "when not" to dribble!

TACTICS OF DRIBBLING

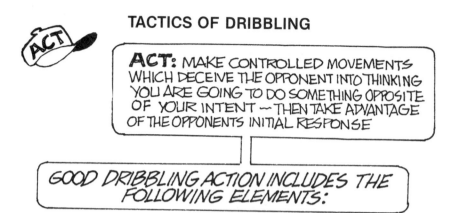

ACT: MAKE CONTROLLED MOVEMENTS WHICH DECEIVE THE OPPONENT INTO THINKING YOU ARE GOING TO DO SOMETHING OPPOSITE OF YOUR INTENT — THEN TAKE ADVANTAGE OF THE OPPONENTS INITIAL RESPONSE

GOOD DRIBBLING ACTION INCLUDES THE FOLLOWING ELEMENTS:

<u>Begin</u> <u>with a feint</u>
(provide false information).

<u>Dribble at a moderate speed</u>
(provide the correct tempo for convincing fakes/feints).

<u>Utilize fakes/feints</u> (get opponent off-balance or wrong footed).

<u>Accelerate past the opponent</u> (explode past off-balanced opponent).

KEY: Keep ball under full control without breaking the rhythm of your stride.

AVOID: Unnecessary confrontations.

TACTICS OF DRIBBLING

PACE: MODERATE RUNNING SPEED PROVIDES THE CORRECT TEMPO FOR FAKES/FEINTS AND OTHER ELEMENTS NECESSARY TO SURPRISE THE OPPONENT.

CONTROL THE PACE BY CHANGING IT. NOT ALL FAST; NOT ALL SLOW

TRAIN TOWARDS: CHANGING PACE OF DRIBBLE AND OBSERVING OPPONENTS RESPONSES.

Congested area:

- Short running stride —
  - allows for better ball control.
  - ease of changing direction of play.

Open space:

- Longer running stride —
  - speed is of the essence.

In both situations be able to change direction and speed quickly while keeping the ball within your playing distance.

Congested area:
    Preparing to turn – Inside of foot

SLOWER DRIBBLE

Turning with the ball using inside of the foot keeps the body between ball and opponent.

Open space:
    Driving thru space – ball on laces.

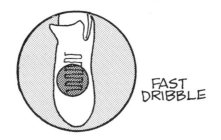

FAST DRIBBLE

Open area:
    Controlled forward dribble – Outside of foot.

MODERATE DRIBBLE

In all situations be able to change direction and speed quickly while keeping the ball within your playing distance.

TACTICS OF DRIBBLING

FAKES/FEINTS: KEEP YOUR OPPONENT GUESSING AS TO YOUR REAL INTENTIONS.

HAVE A VARIETY OF MOVES AVAILABLE WHEN FACED BY DIFFERENT PLAYING SITUATIONS.

Be the master of at least one move--Have others available "just in case".

TRAIN TOWARDS: GETTING OPPONENT OFF-BALANCE BY BODY MOVES:

DIPPING A SHOULDER

"JAB" STEP

FAKING A PASS OR KICK AT THE BALL

USING EYES TO "SELL A DUMMY"

Remember: Any technique will do as long as it leads to success.

For more fake/feint ideas:
FUNDAMENTAL SOCCER-PRACTICE, by Karl Dewazien
pages 42-51
Fred Feathers Publishing Co. ©1985

TACTICS OF DRIBBLING

EXPLODE * AN INCREASED CHANGE OF PACE IS USED TO EXPLOIT YOUR SUCCESSFUL FAKING/FEINTING MOVEMENTS.

DO NOT ALLOW OPPONENT TO RECOVER AND GET A SECOND CHANCE OF GETTING THE BALL OR CATCHING UP WITH YOU.

AVOID: SLOW OR SQUARE MOVEMENTS.

*Explode means from "zero m.p.h." to "after burners".

TACTICS OF DRIBBLING

OPPONENT COMING FROM THE FRONT.

OPTIONS ARE:

① CHANGE OF DIRECTION —BEGIN DRIBBLE WITH A FEINT —PLAY BALL IN A DEFINITE DIRECTION GETTING THE OPPONENT TO MOVE IN THAT DIRECTION—SUDDENLY CHANGE DIRECTION AND SPEED.

Or② ATTACK OPPONENT —BEGIN DRIBBLE WITH A FEINT —APPROACH AT MODERATE SPEED (STRAIGHT AT OPPONENT) —TOTALLY COMMIT OPPONENT TO DEFEND— FORCE OPPONENT BACK ON HIS HEELS WITH A **SUDDEN** MOVE —WHEN OFF BALANCE —**EXPLODE** PAST HIM.

Or ③ UTILIZE FAKE/FEINT~BEGIN DRIBBLE WITH A FEINT~APPROACH AT MODERATE SPEED (STRAIGHT AT THE OPPONENT)~TOTALLY COMMIT OPPONENT TO DEFEND~DO NOT SIGNAL YOUR INTENT, INSTEAD USE **FAKE/FEINT** TO THROW OPPONENT OFF-BALANCE~***EXPLODE*** PAST THE OPPONENT AT THE APPROPRIATE MOMENT.

Remember:

-Focus on the opponents hips and upper legs--<u>look for that definite lean</u>--THEN--play the ball opposite of lean or through the legs--forcing opponent to make a turn in either case.

64

SIDE

OPPONENT AT THE SIDE.

AVOID: PLAYING THE BALL WITH FOOT CLOSEST TO THE OPPONENT.

SCREEN

TRAIN TOWARDS: SHIELDING THE BALL BY KEEPING THE BODY BETWEEN THE OPPONENT AND THE BALL— TOUCH THE BALL WITH FOOT AWAY FROM OPPONENT — GENERALLY WITH "LITTLE TOE" AREA.

LITTLE TOE AREA

TACTICS OF DRIBBLING

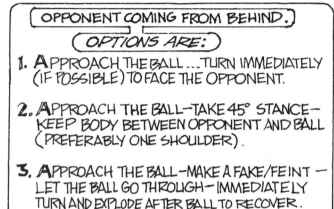

(OPPONENT COMING FROM BEHIND.)

(OPTIONS ARE:)

1. APPROACH THE BALL...TURN IMMEDIATELY (IF POSSIBLE) TO FACE THE OPPONENT.

2. APPROACH THE BALL—TAKE 45° STANCE—KEEP BODY BETWEEN OPPONENT AND BALL (PREFERABLY ONE SHOULDER).

3. APPROACH THE BALL—MAKE A FAKE/FEINT—LET THE BALL GO THROUGH—IMMEDIATELY TURN AND EXPLODE AFTER BALL TO RECOVER.

1.

2.

3.

TACTICS OF DRIBBLING

SCREEN THE BALL:
KEEP THE BODY BETWEEN THE OPPONENT AND THE BALL~PREFERABLY ONE SHOULDER.

TRAIN TOWARDS:
PLAYING BALL WITH FOOT *AWAY* FROM OPPONENT.

Note: While shielding be aware of both ball and opponent--be able to change positions quickly depending on the action/reaction of the opponent.

IMPORTANT:
-Keep the ball moving in a forward motion if at all possible.
-Be able to see the ball and the opponent at the same time!

THE PLAIN FACTS

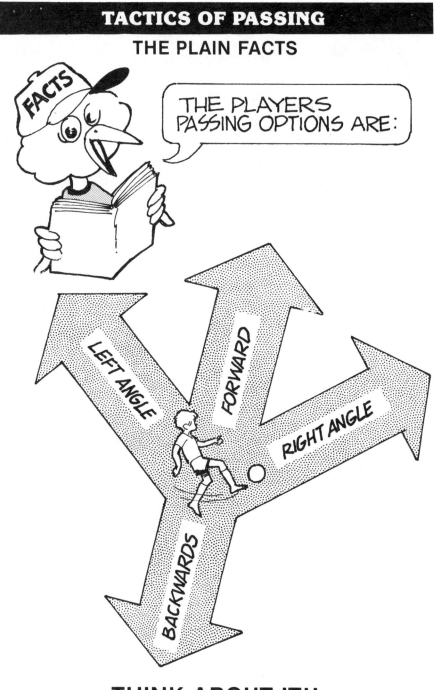

THINK ABOUT IT!!

TACTICS OF PASSING

AN EFFECTIVE ATTACKING PLAYER KNOWS "**WHERE**" TO PASS.

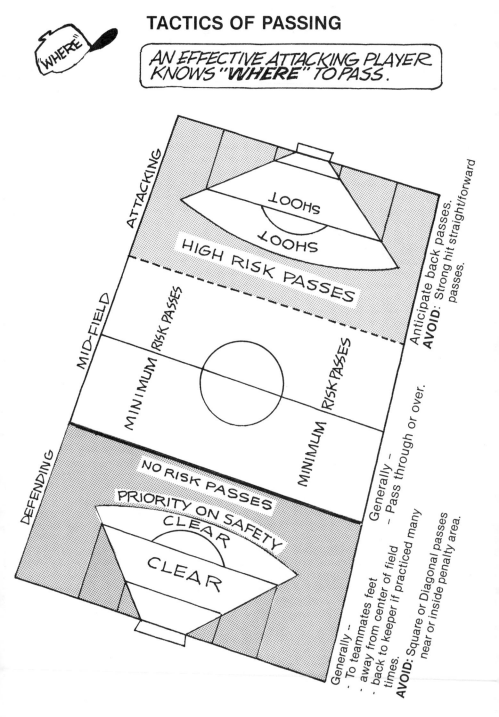

ATTACKING

SHOOT

SHOOT

HIGH RISK PASSES

Anticipate back passes.
AVOID: Strong hit straight/forward passes.

MID-FIELD

MINIMUM RISK PASSES

MINIMUM RISK PASSES

Generally –
– Pass through or over.

DEFENDING

NO RISK PASSES

PRIORITY ON SAFETY

CLEAR

CLEAR

Generally –
- To teammates feet
- away from center of field
- back to keeper if practiced many times.
AVOID: Square or Diagonal passes near or inside penalty area.

TACTICS OF PASSING

AN EFFECTIVE PLAYER KNOWS *"HOW"* TO PASS.

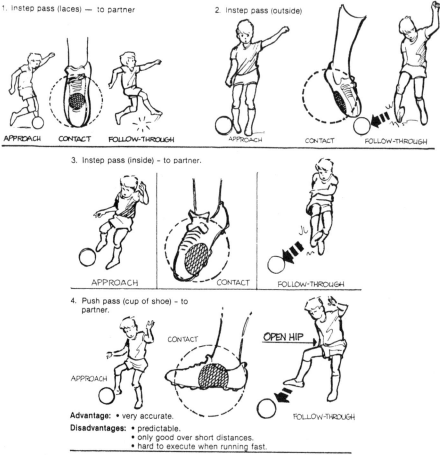

1. Instep pass (laces) — to partner

APPROACH   CONTACT   FOLLOW-THROUGH

2. Instep pass (outside)

APPROACH   CONTACT   FOLLOW-THROUGH

3. Instep pass (inside) – to partner.

APPROACH   CONTACT   FOLLOW-THROUGH

4. Push pass (cup of shoe) – to partner.

APPROACH   CONTACT   OPEN HIP   FOLLOW-THROUGH

Advantage: • very accurate.
Disadvantages: • predictable.
  • only good over short distances.
  • hard to execute when running fast.

KEY: Let them practice what comes natural.

Common to all four passes:
- use relaxed "monkey stance" both knees are slightly bent throughout the passing movement.
- begin each pass by bringing the passing foot behind the plant foot and use a pendulum type swing.
- lock the ankle before contact with the ball.
- Follow through.

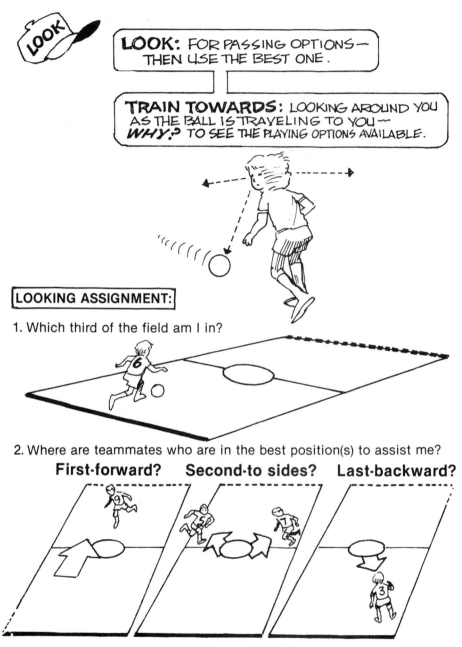

LOOK: FOR PASSING OPTIONS — THEN USE THE BEST ONE.

TRAIN TOWARDS: LOOKING AROUND YOU AS THE BALL IS TRAVELING TO YOU — **WHY?** TO SEE THE PLAYING OPTIONS AVAILABLE.

LOOKING ASSIGNMENT:

1. Which third of the field am I in?

2. Where are teammates who are in the best position(s) to assist me?

First-forward?   Second-to sides?   Last-backward?

IMPORTANT: Make eye contact before the pass.

3. Where are the most threatening opponents?

71

TACTICS OF PASSING

DECIDE: WHAT IS THE BEST PASS TO MAKE ~ IN RELATION TO SUPPORTING TEAMMATE(S) POSITION(S). ALSO CONSIDER OPPONENT'S POSITION.

TRAIN TOWARDS: DECIDE EARLY TO WHO AND AT WHAT TIME PASS IS TO BE MADE.

WHEN POSSIBLE MENTALLY SELECT YOUR TARGET TEAMMATE AS BALL APPROACHES YOU.

DECIDING ASSIGNMENT:

- First, is it possible to pass the ball forward to a teammate?
- Will I have to pass to a teammate on the side or behind me?
- Will I first time pass ball to teammate?
- Do I have time to control and then pass?
- Will I have to control and dribble and then pass?

An effective player knows "WHEN" and "WHEN NOT" to pass.

72

TACTICS OF PASSING

ACT: MAKE EYE CONTACT WITH A TEAMMATE BEFORE PASSING TO HIM.

MAKE THE FORWARD PASS YOUR FIRST PRIORITY.

NOTE: If there is an open man ahead of you – pass the ball.

TRAIN TOWARDS: MAKING PASSES THAT THE RECEIVER CAN BRING UNDER HIS CONTROL IMMEDIATELY.

| ACTION ASSIGNMENT |

- Be accurate--the ball must reach its intended target.

- Pass so teammate can control, shoot, pass or dribble without breaking stride if required.

- **EXECUTE ALL PASSES IN RELATION TO THE RECEIVERS KNOWN** SKILL LEVEL.

TACTICS OF PASSING

MOVE: AFTER PASS IS MADE RE-POSITION YOURSELF TO FURTHER SUPPORT THE RECEIVER.

TRAIN TOWARDS: *PASS AND SUPPORT YOUR PASS.*

AVOID: PASSING THE BALL AND THEN ADMIRING THE PASS FROM A STATIONARY POSITION.

MOVING ASSIGNMENT:

Pass-and-run...

TACTICS OF PASSING

DISGUISE: MAKE THE INTENT OF YOUR PASS UNCLEAR TO THE OPPONENT.

"DON'T TELEGRAPH INTENT."

AVOID: PASSING IN THE DIRECTION YOUR BODY POSITION INDICATES.

TRAIN TOWARDS:

LOOK IN ONE DIRECTION, PASS TO THE OPPOSITE.

POINT IN ONE DIRECTION, PASS TO THE OPPOSITE.

DRIBBLE IN ONE DIRECTION, PASS TO THE OPPOSITE.

FEINT/FAKE IN ONE DIRECTION, PASS TO THE OPPOSITE.

Note: Keep the element of surprise as your weapon.

75

TACTICS OF PASSING

PASS TO FOOT: PLAY BALL TO TEAM-MATES *"FREE"* FOOT, THAT IS, FOOT AWAY FROM THREATENING OPPONENT.

IMPORTANT: Pass <u>Hard to Feet</u>-for quick control and to prevent opponent's reaction.

AVOID: *PASSING TO FOOT NEAREST OPPONENT.*

Note: Ball placement to receiver should communicate where threatening opponent is positioned or moving from.

TACTICS OF PASSING

LEAD PASS: PLAYING BALL INTO *"FREE"* SPACE TELLS PLAYER WHERE TO RUN AND WHERE OPPONENTS ARE **NOT** POSITIONED.

IMPORTANT: Pass <u>Soft to Space</u> — Pacing the pass so that team-mate and ball arrive at the same time. Make pass so that receiver does not have to break stride.

LEAD PASS NOTES:

- Should be made past opponents
- Ideally, perfected in the attacking third but can be used anywhere.
- Receiver should continually check to see if he is off-side--verbal call from teammates when necessary.

COMBINATION PLAY

COMBINATION PLAY SHOULD BE VIEWED AS CLEARLY DEFINED *PATTERNS OF PLAYERS WORKING TOGETHER*.

for example:

SIDE BY SIDE PATTERNS INCLUDE:

1. **Square Pass** across the face of the opponent.

PASS HARD TO FEET

2. **Lead Pass** behind the opponent.

PASS SOFT TO SPACE

3. Pass and run an **Overlap** on the man receiving the pass.

4. "U" turn **Take-Over.**

COMBINATION PLAY

IN-TANDEM PATTERNS INCLUDE:"GIVE AND GO", "WALL PASS", "PULL-SERIES" AND "TAKE-OVER".

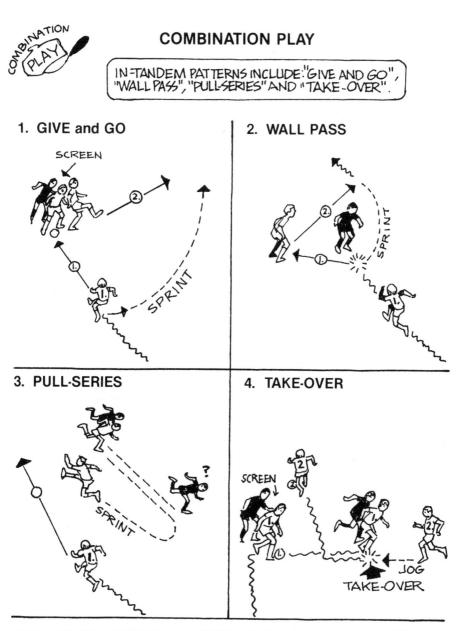

1. GIVE and GO

SCREEN

SPRINT

2. WALL PASS

SPRINT

3. PULL-SERIES

SPRINT

?

4. TAKE-OVER

SCREEN

JOG

TAKE-OVER

THE AIM OF EACH PATTERN IS TO BEAT THE OPPONENT SO THAT THE OFFENSIVE PLAYER IS IN A MORE ADVANTAGEOUS POSITION TO ADVANCE, PASS-OFF OR SHOOT.

Master one "Combination Pattern" before introducing the next.

COMBINATION PLAY

GIVE AND **GO**
UNDER THESE CONDITIONS
THE "GIVE AND GO"
IS EXECUTED:

DRIBBLER/PASSER/RUNNER ("GIVER") (G)
TEAMMATE ("RELEASER") (R)
DEFENDER MARKING THE "RELEASER" ("OPPONENT") (O)

To execute properly:

1. "Giver" passes to "releasers" foot.

2. "Giver" sprints in quick support of the ball-in a wide angular fashion.

3. "Releaser" screens the ball until the proper moment to give ball back.

4. "Releaser" plays ball into "givers" running path.

———— KEY POINTS: ————

GIVER
- Eye contact with front player "releaser".
- Pass ball to feet of "releaser".
- Quick arching burst past "releaser".
- Verbal call (when possible)

RELEASER
- Screen ball from opponent.
- Wait for "giver" to run.
- Pass in front of "giver".
- Immediately support newly created situation.

●●●●●●●●●●●●●●●●●●●●●●●●●● OPTION: ●●●●●●●●●●●●●●●●●●●●●●●●●●●●

"Releaser" keeps/advances **the ball** when "Opponent" anticipates play.

80

COMBINATION PLAY

WALL-PASS: UNDER THESE CONDITIONS THE WALL-PASS IS EXECUTED.

TWO OFFENSIVE PLAYERS: 1. PLAYER WITH BALL ("DRIBBLER") (D) 2. SUPPORT PLAYER ("WALL") (W) **ONE DEFENSIVE PLAYER:** ("OPPONENT") (O)

FINER POINTS OF THE WALL PASS:

1. "Wall" calls for the play by sprinting toward the ball into a "Square Pass" position.
   – "Dribbler" goes straight at opponent.

2. Eye contact between "Dribbler" and "Wall".
   – "Wall" anticipates first time return pass.

3. "Dribbler" square passes, generally using outside of foot.

4. "Dribbler" explodes around "Opponent" to regain ball possession.
   – "Wall" gives <u>first time pass</u> behind "Opponent" for "Dribbler" to receive in unbroken stride.

KEY POINTS

Dribbler-
 –Go straight at the "opponent".
 –Approach at a controlled pace.
 –Give a properly paced accurate pass to "wall" feet.
 –Explode past "opponent" opposite of pass
 –Retrieve return pass.

Wall-
 –Usually calls for the ball verbally
 –Sprint into a positive position right or left of the opponent
 –Prepare for first time return
 –Pass (behind "opponent")
 –Move to again support your teammate as he advances

WALL-PASS OPTIONS

> **PLAYER WITH THE BALL ("DRIBBLER") (D) HAS TWO OPTIONS:**

1. To **keep the ball**
   -using "Wall" as decoy

2. To **part with the ball**
   -using "wall"

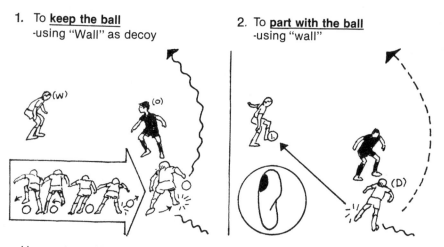

He must use his judgement as to which is more beneficial at that moment.

●●

> **PLAYER WITHOUT THE BALL ("WALL") (W) SHOULD UNDERSTAND HIS TWO OPTIONS:**

1. To **return ball** immediately to dribbler or other teammate.

2. To **keep the ball** and advance.

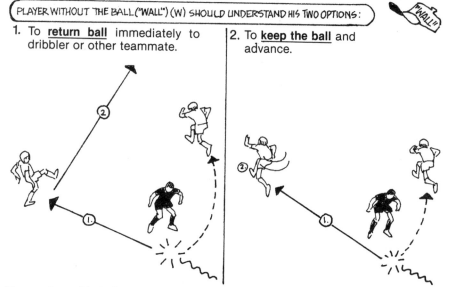

He must use his judgement as to which is more beneficial at that moment.

All players on the team must realize that the options available depend on the opponents actions/reactions in each particular situation.

COMBINATION PLAY

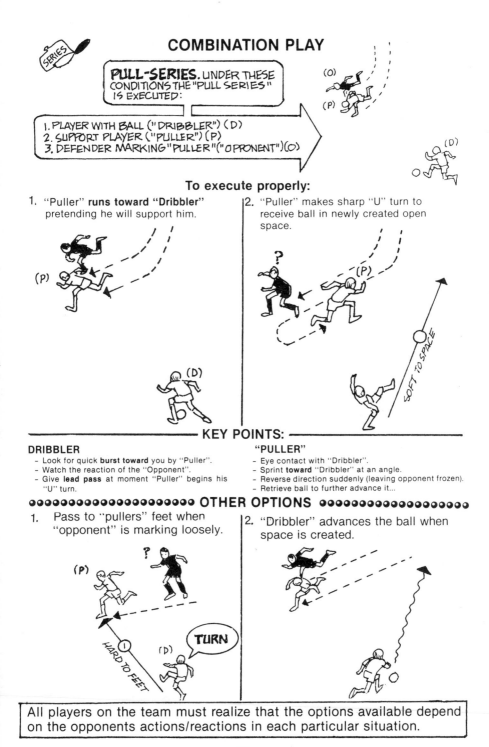

PULL-SERIES. UNDER THESE CONDITIONS THE "PULL SERIES" IS EXECUTED:

1. PLAYER WITH BALL ("DRIBBLER") (D)
2. SUPPORT PLAYER ("PULLER") (P)
3. DEFENDER MARKING "PULLER" ("OPPONENT") (O)

To execute properly:

1. "Puller" **runs toward "Dribbler"** pretending he will support him.

2. "Puller" makes sharp "U" turn to receive ball in newly created open space.

SOFT TO SPACE

━━ KEY POINTS: ━━

DRIBBLER
- Look for quick **burst toward** you by "Puller".
- Watch the reaction of the "Opponent".
- Give **lead pass** at moment "Puller" begins his "U" turn.

"PULLER"
- Eye contact with "Dribbler".
- Sprint **toward** "Dribbler" at an angle.
- Reverse direction suddenly (leaving opponent frozen).
- Retrieve ball to further advance it...

●●●●●●●●●●●●●●●●●●●● OTHER OPTIONS ●●●●●●●●●●●●●●●●●●●●

1. Pass to "pullers" feet when "opponent" is marking loosely.

HARD TO FEET

TURN

2. "Dribbler" advances the ball when space is created.

All players on the team must realize that the options available depend on the opponents actions/reactions in each particular situation.

PULL-SERIES OPTIONS

PULL-RETURN

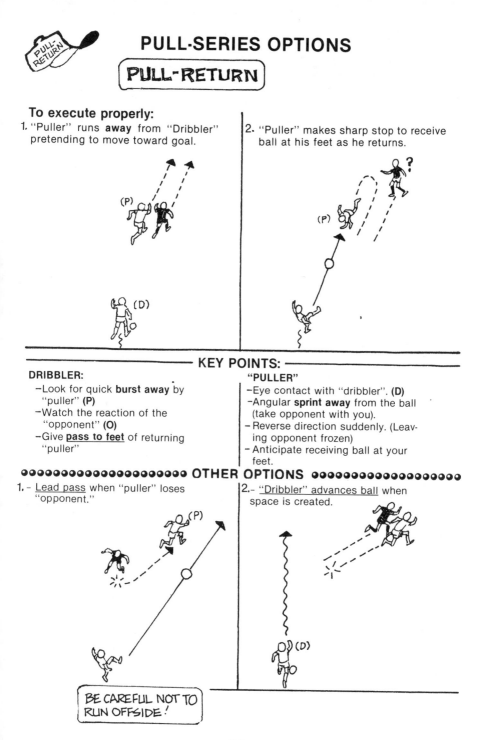

To execute properly:

1. "Puller" runs **away** from "Dribbler" pretending to move toward goal.

2. "Puller" makes sharp stop to receive ball at his feet as he returns.

(P)

(D)

(P)

?

--- KEY POINTS: ---

DRIBBLER:
- Look for quick **burst away** by "puller" **(P)**
- Watch the reaction of the "opponent" **(O)**
- Give **pass to feet** of returning "puller"

"PULLER"
- Eye contact with "dribbler". **(D)**
- Angular **sprint away** from the ball (take opponent with you).
- Reverse direction suddenly. (Leaving opponent frozen)
- Anticipate receiving ball at your feet.

●●●●●●●●●●●●●●●●●●●●● OTHER OPTIONS ●●●●●●●●●●●●●●●●●●●●●

1. - Lead pass when "puller" loses "opponent."

(P)

2. - "Dribbler" advances ball when space is created.

(D)

BE CAREFUL NOT TO RUN OFFSIDE!

84

PULL-SERIES OPTIONS

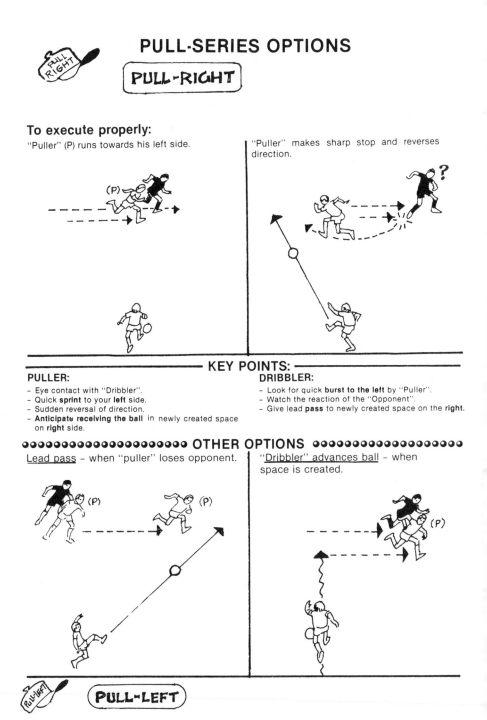

PULL-RIGHT

To execute properly:

"Puller" (P) runs towards his left side.

"Puller" makes sharp stop and reverses direction.

KEY POINTS:

PULLER:
- Eye contact with "Dribbler".
- Quick **sprint** to your **left** side.
- Sudden reversal of direction.
- **Anticipate receiving the ball** in newly created space on **right** side.

DRIBBLER:
- Look for quick **burst to the left** by "Puller".
- Watch the reaction of the "Opponent".
- Give lead **pass** to newly created space on the **right**.

●●●●●●●●●●●●●●●●●●●●●● OTHER OPTIONS ●●●●●●●●●●●●●●●●●●●●●●

Lead pass – when "puller" loses opponent.

"Dribbler" advances ball – when space is created.

PULL-LEFT

Same instructions — opposite side.

COMBINATION PLAY

TAKE-OVER UNDER THESE CONDITIONS THE "TAKE-OVER" IS EXECUTED.

1. PLAYER SCREENING THE BALL ("DRIBBLER") **(D)**
2. SUPPORT PLAYER ("TAKER") **(T)**
3. DEFENDER MARKING THE "DRIBBLER" ("OPPONENT") **(O)**

To execute properly:

1. Having been denied forward motion the "dribbler" signals for the "take-over" by screening the ball.

2. "Dribbler" moves across the field and "opponents" path towards "taker".

SCREEN

SHALLOW JOG

3. "Dribbler" stops or lays the ball at "takers" foot as "taker" moves in opposite horizontal path.

4. "Taker" advances ball in newly created direction.

RIGHT FOOT LEAVE *

RIGHT FOOT TAKE *

?

═══ KEY POINTS: ═══

DRIBBLER:
Screen the ball ("away foot" carries the ball).
Dribble towards teammate.
Eye contact with teammate.
Stop or leave ball for teammate to take-over.
*Important: Stop or leave ball — Do not pass it.

"TAKER"
Eye contact with "dribbler".
Moderate running speed toward "dribbler".
*Take over ball with same foot as "dribbler"
*Example : "Dribbler" moving ball with right foot — Take ball with your right foot.

Explosive movement of ball behind/past the opponent.

TAKE-OVER OPTION:
PLAYER SCREENING THE BALL
"DRIBBLER" KEEPS THE BALL.

1. Having been denied forward motion, the "Dribbler" signals for the "Take-Over" by screening the ball.

2. "Dribbler" moves across the field and "opponents" path towards "taker".

3. "Dribbler" **keeps ball** when "Opponent" anticipates the play.

4. "Dribbler" advances ball in newly created direction.

All players on the team must realize that the options available depend on the opponents actions in each particular situation.

Do not forget that **"EYE CONTACT"** and **"MOVEMENT"** are both essential in "**Calling**" for the ball. **Not just yelling.** Sometimes the loud call is to attract an opponent and not the ball.

COMBINATION PLAY NOTES–Continued

IN ADDITION: SOME TEAMS DEVELOP PHYSICAL MOVEMENTS TO SIGNAL UPCOMING PATTERN AND ITS OPTIONS ...FOR EXAMPLE: POINTING, ETC.

Examples:

1. GIVE and GO

"RELEASER" POINTS TO TOUCH LINE

2. WALL PASS

"WALL" POINTS AT OPPONENT

3. PULL

"PULLER" POINTS TO TOES

4. TAKE-OVER

"TAKER" POINTS AT HIMSELF

There are no rules for how information is to be given.

IF IT WORKS – THEN IT IS RIGHT!

THE ULTIMATE AIM IS: TO HAVE PLAYERS "KNOW" EACH OTHER WELL ENOUGH TO BE ABLE TO "READ" THE OTHERS INTENTIONS WITHOUT SIGNALS.

It is this authors belief that **the key** to successful combination play begins with the **training of the support player who initiates the play** through proper communication, positioning, ball skill and anticipation.

DEFENDING
THE INDIVIDUALS ROLE:
THE PLAIN FACTS:

When a team loses ball possession **each individual becomes a defender** with the following OBJECTIVES:

1. INTERCEPT

2. SHEPHERD   3. TACKLE

WIN BACK THE BALL!
THINK ABOUT IT!!!

DEFENSIVE TACTICS · INDIVIDUAL
RUN, BALL SIDE & GOALSIDE

KEEP THE OPPONENT UNDER CONSTANT PHYSICAL AND MENTAL PRESSURE AND ALL OTHER MEMBERS PREVENT OPPONENT FROM RECEIVING THE BALL.

Correct way to mark opponent who is not in possession.

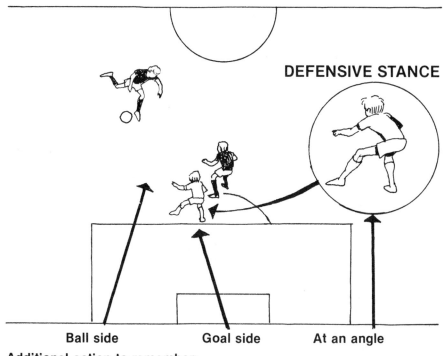

DEFENSIVE STANCE

| Ball side | Goal side | At an angle |

Additional action to remember:

See both the ball and the opponent at the same time.

Keep a safe distance so that ground can be covered prior to ball reaching opponent.

The closer to your goal the tighter the marking.

AVOID: Total concentration on just one player - be available for changes and emergencies.

KEEP THE OPPONENT UNDER CONSTANT PHYSICAL AND MENTAL PRESSURE THROUGH PROPER MARKING.

– Goal side but not ball side

– Too far away

– Directly behind

Interception is your best defensive weapon – if you are able to cut-off the pass — DO SO!

DEFENSIVE TACTICS · INDIVIDUAL

IF YOU ARE ABLE TO <u>INTERCEPT</u> THE BALL **DO SO!**

IF YOU ARE NOT ABLE TO INTERCEPT THE BALL THEN AN EFFECTIVE DEFENDER KNOWS "**WHEN**" TO WIN THE BALL.

1. RUN QUICKLY WHILE THE BALL IS TRAVELING.

2. TIME YOUR RUN SO THAT YOU REACH THE ATTACKER AT THE SAME MOMENT THE BALL ARRIVES.

3. TACKLE AT THE MOMENT ATTACKER IS RECEIVING THE BALL, JUST BEFORE HE HAS CONTROLLED IT.

Important — the player nearest the man receiving the ball does the job!

93

DEFENSIVE TACTICS · INDIVIDUAL

PREVENT TURNING

IF THE OPPONENT HAS GAINED CONTROL OF THE BALL *THEN* AN EFFECTIVE DEFENDER *PREVENTS* THE OPPONENT FROM *TURNING* TOWARD HIS GOAL.

"Glide" into the
DEFENSIVE STANCE

Play <u>behind</u> – far enough to see top of ball.

<u>Watch the ball</u> not hips or shoulders because a fake/feint may throw you off-balance.

Go for the ball (<u>tackle</u>) as the attacker goes into a <u>half-turn</u>. (Tackle at mid-turn)

Keep opponent playing in front of you!

<u>Common mistakes:</u>

• Coming too fast and too hard   • Marking too close

IF THE OPPONENT HAS GAINED CONTROL OF THE BALL AND SUCCESSFULLY TURNED *THEN* AN EFFECTIVE DEFENDER KNOWS "**HOW**" TO WIN THE BALL.

ALL DEFENSIVE MOVES ARE INITIATED FROM THE *"DEFENSIVE STANCE"*.

THIS POSITION SHOULD BE INSTINCTIVELY ASSUMED WHENEVER THE OPPONENT GAINS BALL POSSESSION.

The
**DEFENSIVE
STANCE**
requires that:

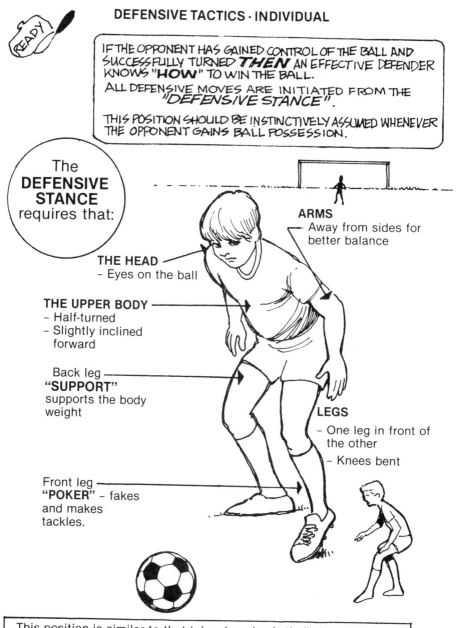

ARMS
– Away from sides for
better balance

THE HEAD
– Eyes on the ball

THE UPPER BODY
– Half-turned
– Slightly inclined
forward

Back leg
"SUPPORT"
supports the body
weight

LEGS
– One leg in front of
the other
– Knees bent

Front leg
"POKER" – fakes
and makes
tackles.

This position is similar to that taken by a basketball player or boxer.

Important:
– Be balanced by playing on the balls of the feet not flatfooted
– Be mentally alert and ready to move in any direction.

DEFENSIVE TACTICS – INDIVIDUAL
DEFENSIVE STANCE

ADOPT THE *"DEFENSIVE STANCE"* WHICH ALLOWS FOR QUICK TURNING BY MOVING BACK THE FOOT THAT IS ON THE SIDE FROM WHICH THE *"DRIBBLER"* IS APPROACHING.

Example:
"Dribbler" approaching right side – right foot goes back.

"Dribbler" approaching left side – left foot goes back.

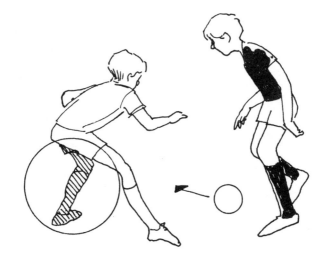

Place body weight on back foot — Leaving front foot "poker" free to manuever. Shuffle feet — without ever lifting them from the ground.

"**POKER**" FAKES ATTEMPTS AT THE BALL.

Force dribbler to watch the ball — Make the dribbler play defensive, that is — protecting the ball from you.

Poking at the ball makes the dribbler look down! This reduces his field of vision and makes it more difficult to continue to dribble or pass

Should the dribbler lose temporary control of the ball — use the "poker" to steal the ball away.

AVOID LUNGING AT THE BALL!

"POKER" MOVES

IF DRIBBLER IS ABLE TO CHANGE DIRECTION, THE "**POKER**" MOVES IN AN ARCH FOLLOWING THE BALL AND AUTOMATICALLY BECOMES THE ***BACKFOOT.***

Important: The legs should **never** cross when the opponent changes direction.

DEFENSIVE TACTICS - INDIVIDUAL

POINTS TO REMEMBER WHEN GETTING INTO *"DEFENSIVE STANCE."*

Time to run quickly is while the ball is traveling to your opponent.

If interception is not possible slow down run by dropping buttocks (bending knees) and "gliding" into **DEFENSIVE STANCE** keeping both feet moving.

Get within "striking" distance of the player with the ball (Ideally— two yards from the ball).

Overplay the dribbler—that is, play off his shoulder to make play predictible in one direction.

Nose even with dribbler's shoulder.

DEFENSIVE TACTICS - INDIVIDUAL

POINTS TO REMEMBER WHEN IN THE *"DEFENSIVE STANCE"*.

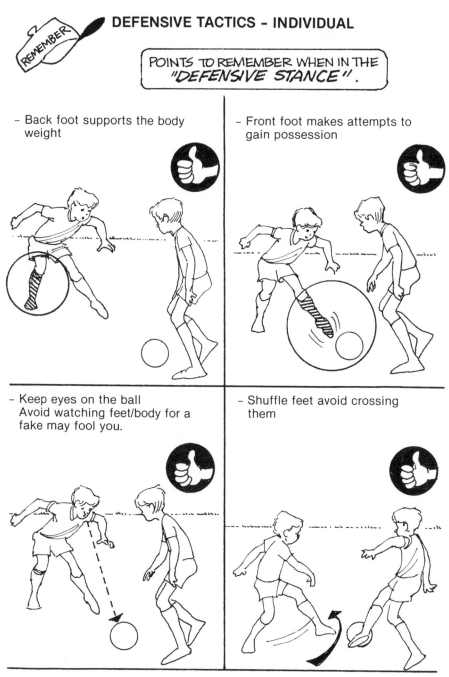

- Back foot supports the body weight

- Front foot makes attempts to gain possession

- Keep eyes on the ball
  Avoid watching feet/body for a fake may fool you.

- Shuffle feet avoid crossing them

MOST IMPORTANT — KEEP YOUR BODY BETWEEN THE BALL AND THE GOAL . . .

DEFENSIVE TACTICS - INDIVIDUAL
SHEPHERDING

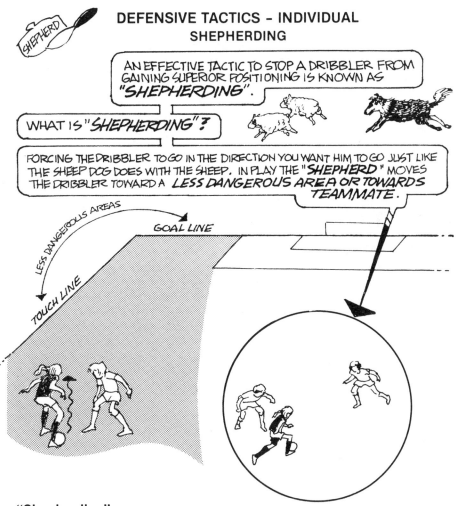

AN EFFECTIVE TACTIC TO STOP A DRIBBLER FROM GAINING SUPERIOR POSITIONING IS KNOWN AS *"SHEPHERDING"*.

WHAT IS *"SHEPHERDING"*?

FORCING THE DRIBBLER TO GO IN THE DIRECTION YOU WANT HIM TO GO JUST LIKE THE SHEEP DOG DOES WITH THE SHEEP. IN PLAY THE *"SHEPHERD"* MOVES THE DRIBBLER TOWARD A *LESS DANGEROUS AREA OR TOWARDS TEAMMATE*.

LESS DANGEROUS AREAS

GOAL LINE

TOUCH LINE

"Shepherding"—
- Allows for minimum errors by the individual defending.
- May result in stopping the game—ball out of bounds.
- May result in gaining ball possession—dribbling mistakes.
- Should slow the dribbler down—delay.

Players need to decide whether to "shepherd" dribbler or use possibly risky tackling techniques.

DEFENSIVE TACTICS - INDIVIDUAL

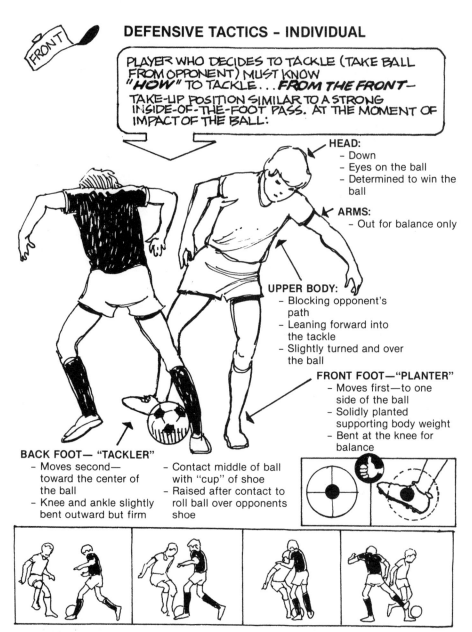

FRONT

PLAYER WHO DECIDES TO TACKLE (TAKE BALL FROM OPPONENT) MUST KNOW *"HOW"* TO TACKLE... **FROM THE FRONT** – TAKE-UP POSITION SIMILAR TO A STRONG INSIDE-OF-THE-FOOT PASS. AT THE MOMENT OF IMPACT OF THE BALL:

HEAD:
- Down
- Eyes on the ball
- Determined to win the ball

ARMS:
- Out for balance only

UPPER BODY:
- Blocking opponent's path
- Leaning forward into the tackle
- Slightly turned and over the ball

FRONT FOOT—"PLANTER"
- Moves first—to one side of the ball
- Solidly planted supporting body weight
- Bent at the knee for balance

BACK FOOT— "TACKLER"
- Moves second— toward the center of the ball
- Knee and ankle slightly bent outward but firm

- Contact middle of ball with "cup" of shoe
- Raised after contact to roll ball over opponents shoe

REMEMBER:
- Do not lunge at the ball
- Make contact on the ball when dribbler is temporarily out of possession
- Realize that you will not always win the ball
- Be satisfied to occassionally poke or kick the ball away

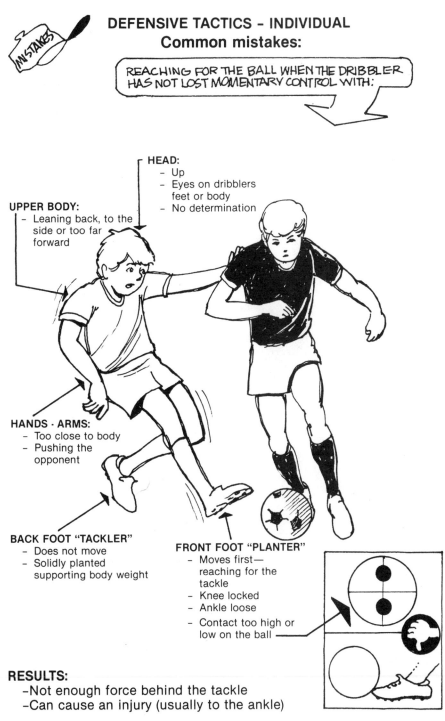

DEFENSIVE TACTICS - INDIVIDUAL
Common mistakes:

MISTAKES

REACHING FOR THE BALL WHEN THE DRIBBLER HAS NOT LOST MOMENTARY CONTROL WITH:

HEAD:
- Up
- Eyes on dribblers feet or body
- No determination

UPPER BODY:
- Leaning back, to the side or too far forward

HANDS - ARMS:
- Too close to body
- Pushing the opponent

BACK FOOT "TACKLER"
- Does not move
- Solidly planted supporting body weight

FRONT FOOT "PLANTER"
- Moves first— reaching for the tackle
- Knee locked
- Ankle loose
- Contact too high or low on the ball

RESULTS:
- Not enough force behind the tackle
- Can cause an injury (usually to the ankle)

PLAYER WHO DECIDES TO TACKLE (TAKE BALL FROM OPPONENT) MUST KNOW *"HOW"* TO TACKLE ...
FROM THE SIDE –
FIRST OBJECTIVE: *DO NOT LET DRIBBLER GET AHEAD OF YOU.*
SECOND OBJECTIVE: *SLOW DOWN THE DRIBBLER.*
THIRD OBJECTIVE: *USE SLIDE TACKLE ONLY AS A LAST RESORT.*

"POKE AWAY".

USE **NEAREST FOOT** TO DRIBBLER – WHEN BALL IS AHEAD OF HIM – AND KICK THE BALL AWAY.

DEFENSIVE TACTICS – INDIVIDUAL

"SHOULDER-TO-SHOULDER CHARGE"

LEAN ON YOUR OPPONENT'S SHOULDER AS YOU ATTEMPT TO PLAY THE BALL.

– Generally used when dribbler is on touchline side.

– Seldom used when dribbler is goal side.

Avoid use of the lower arm or hands.

Avoid bringing elbow away from body.

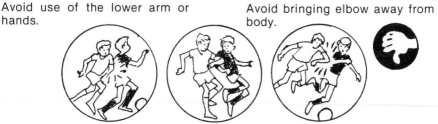

DEFENSIVE TACTICS – INDIVIDUAL
PIVOT TACKLE

SHOULD THE DRIBBLER BE AHEAD, YOU MAY DECIDE TO USE THE "*PIVOT TACKLE*" WHICH CONSISTS OF:

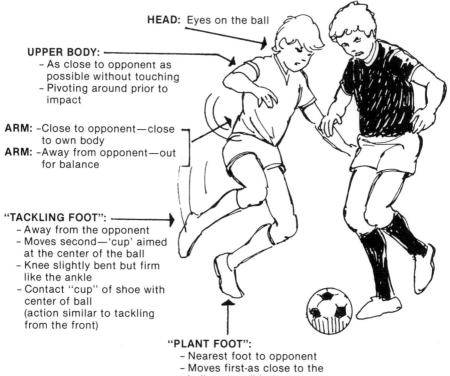

HEAD: Eyes on the ball

UPPER BODY:
- As close to opponent as possible without touching
- Pivoting around prior to impact

ARM: –Close to opponent—close to own body
ARM: –Away from opponent—out for balance

"TACKLING FOOT":
- Away from the opponent
- Moves second—'cup' aimed at the center of the ball
- Knee slightly bent but firm like the ankle
- Contact "cup" of shoe with center of ball
(action similar to tackling from the front)

"PLANT FOOT":
- Nearest foot to opponent
- Moves first-as close to the ball as possible (even or slightly in front)
- Semi-turned to allow for upcoming pivot
- Knee slightly bent for balance

Important:
--Make contact with the ball before touching the opponent
--Stay on your feet

DEFENSIVE TACTICS · INDIVIDUAL
DEFENDING THIRD:

APPLY THE GREATEST AMOUNT OF PRESSURE ON THE BALL WITH THE LEAST AMOUNT OF RISK. *NO FOULS!*

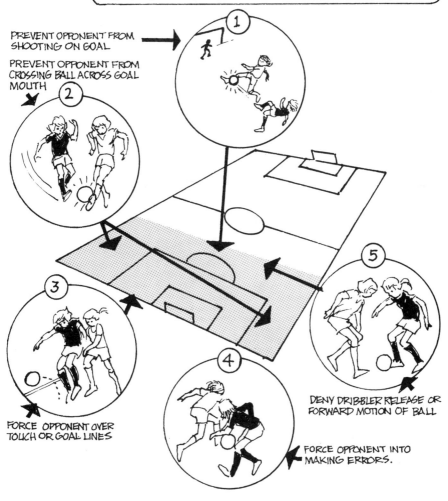

PREVENT OPPONENT FROM SHOOTING ON GOAL

PREVENT OPPONENT FROM CROSSING BALL ACROSS GOAL MOUTH

FORCE OPPONENT OVER TOUCH OR GOAL LINES

DENY DRIBBLER RELEASE OR FORWARD MOTION OF BALL

FORCE OPPONENT INTO MAKING ERRORS.

MARKING – THE CLOSER THE GOAL, THE TIGHTER THE MARKING.

– ELIMINATE *EVERY THREATENING ATTACKER* BY ANY FAIR MEANS AVAILABLE.

TACKLING – STRONG, HARD AND ACCURATE BUT NOT RECKLESS.

DEFENSIVE TACTICS - INDIVIDUAL
MID-FIELD THIRD:

> APPLY THE GREATEST AMOUNT OF PRESSURE ON
> THE BALL WITH A MINIMUM AMOUNT OF RISK.
> —*MAKE PLAY PREDICTABLE!*

- **PREVENT** the forward/through pass.

- **DELAY** the attack - Slow them down!

1. Toward the touch line.   2. Toward your teammate(s).

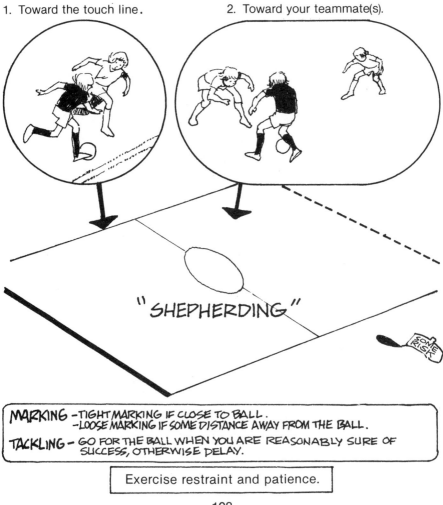

"SHEPHERDING"

MARKING –TIGHT MARKING IF CLOSE TO BALL.
  –LOOSE MARKING IF SOME DISTANCE AWAY FROM THE BALL.

TACKLING – GO FOR THE BALL WHEN YOU ARE REASONABLY SURE OF
  SUCCESS, OTHERWISE DELAY.

Exercise restraint and patience.

DEFENSIVE TACTICS · INDIVIDUAL
ATTACKING THIRD:

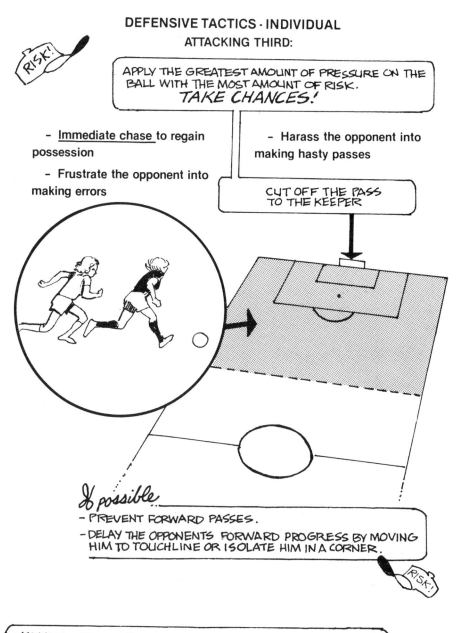

APPLY THE GREATEST AMOUNT OF PRESSURE ON THE BALL WITH THE MOST AMOUNT OF RISK.
TAKE CHANCES!

- <u>Immediate chase</u> to regain possession

- Frustrate the opponent into making errors

- Harass the opponent into making hasty passes

CUT OFF THE PASS TO THE KEEPER

If possible
- PREVENT FORWARD PASSES.
- DELAY THE OPPONENTS FORWARD PROGRESS BY MOVING HIM TO TOUCHLINE OR ISOLATE HIM IN A CORNER.

MARKING - TIGHT MARKING IF CLOSE TO BALL.
- LEAVE NO OPPONENT OPEN FOR A DIRECT PASS

TACKLING - USE ANY LEGAL MEANS AVAILABLE TO REGAIN POSSESSION.

TAKE SOME CHANCES!

DEFENSIVE – TEAM TACTICS

WHEN DOES DEFENSIVE "TEAM" TACTICS BEGIN?

AT THE MOMENT THE BALL CHANGES POSSESSION.

WHAT DEFENSIVE ACTION CAN "TEAM" APPLY?

1. IMMEDIATE CHASE

2. ORGANIZED RETREAT

3. FULL RETREAT

THINK ABOUT IT!

DEFENSIVE — TEAM TACTICS

IN APPLYING "TEAM" DEFENSE PLAYERS NEED TO BE TAUGHT "HOW" OPPONENTS ARE MARKED. FOR YOUNGER CHILDREN THEY SHOULD BE ACQUAINTED WITH THESE FOUR APPROACHES:

1. MAN-ON-MAN MARKING

Each player has a specific opponent to cover the entire game.

2. ZONE MARKING

Each player has tunnel/channel and is responsible for any opponent who enters this area.

CHANNELS → LEFT GOAL RIGHT

3. COMBINATION MARKING

Man-on-Man with their outstanding player. Zone for the rest of the team.

4. NEAREST MAN MARKING

(most difficult to teach)
Each Player is responsible for marking the opponent who is nearest to him when opponent gains ball possession.

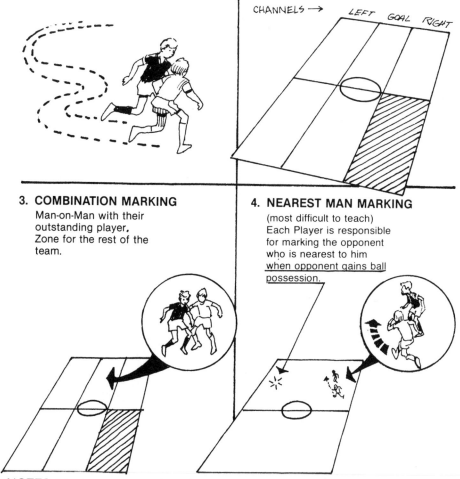

NOTES: Master one type of marking before introducing the next.
Make certain team knows what type of marking they are expected to use.

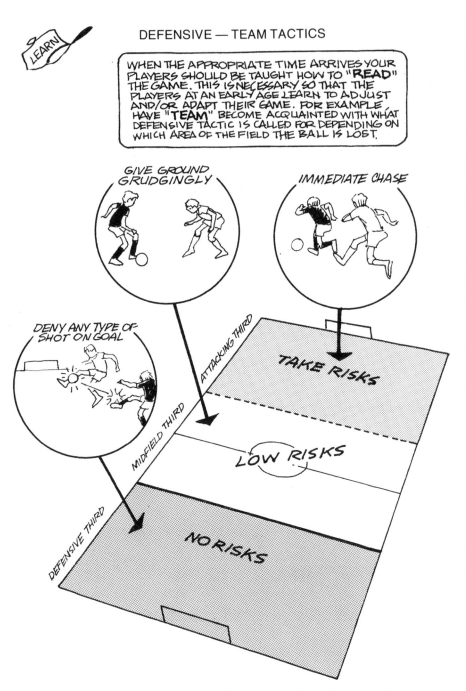

WHEN THE APPROPRIATE TIME ARRIVES YOUR PLAYERS SHOULD BE TAUGHT HOW TO "**READ**" THE GAME. THIS IS NECESSARY SO THAT THE PLAYERS AT AN EARLY AGE LEARN TO ADJUST AND/OR ADAPT THEIR GAME. FOR EXAMPLE, HAVE "**TEAM**" BECOME ACQUAINTED WITH WHAT DEFENSIVE TACTIC IS CALLED FOR DEPENDING ON WHICH AREA OF THE FIELD THE BALL IS LOST.

GIVE GROUND GRUDGINGLY

IMMEDIATE CHASE

DENY ANY TYPE OF SHOT ON GOAL

ATTACKING THIRD

TAKE RISKS

MIDFIELD THIRD

LOW RISKS

DEFENSIVE THIRD

NO RISKS

Player should be taught to be aware of what he and each teammate are supposed to do in any given game situation.

DEFENSIVE — TEAM TACTICS
IMMEDIATE PRESSURE
Can be compared to "full court press" in basketball.

THE PURPOSE OF "**IMMEDIATE PRESSURE**" IS TO PREVENT
OPPONENT FROM GAINING A MORE ADVANTAGEOUS FIELD POSITION
WHICH COULD ALLOW A SCORING OPPORTUNITY.

How do you teach "immediate pressure"?

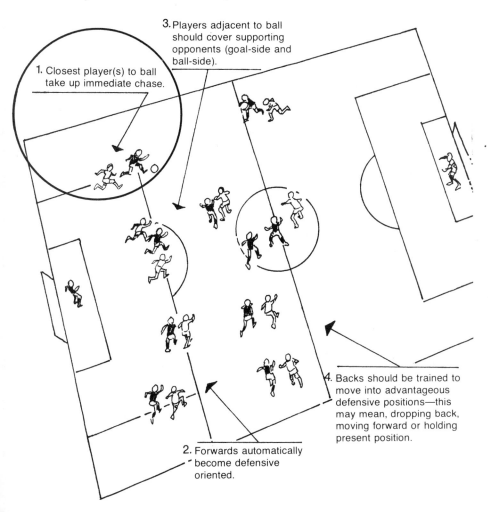

3. Players adjacent to ball should cover supporting opponents (goal-side and ball-side).

1. Closest player(s) to ball take up immediate chase.

4. Backs should be trained to move into advantageous defensive positions—this may mean, dropping back, moving forward or holding present position.

2. Forwards automatically become defensive oriented.

This seems to be the most popular youth tactic but requires absolute commitment from all team members.

ORGANIZED RETREAT
Giving ground grudgingly.

> THE PURPOSE OF "ORGANIZED RETREAT" IS TO SLOW DOWN OPPONENT—GAIN BALL POSSESSION AT A LATER TIME.

How do you teach "organized retreat"?

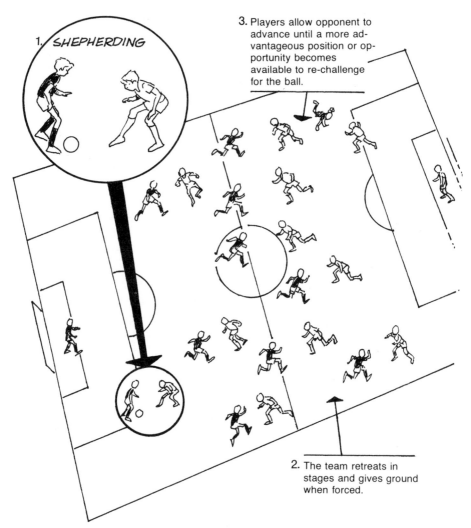

1. SHEPHERDING

3. Players allow opponent to advance until a more advantageous position or opportunity becomes available to re-challenge for the ball.

2. The team retreats in stages and gives ground when forced.

FULL RETREAT

Can be compared to "half court press" in basketball.

THE PURPOSE OF "**FULL RETREAT**" IS TO CUT-OFF ALL
AVENUES TO THE GOAL MOUTH IN ONES OWN HALF OF THE
FIELD. THIS TACTIC SHOULD BE USED WHEN OPPONENT
IS CLEARLY SUPERIOR.

How do you teach "full retreat"?

1. Train **all** players to drop back, on pre-arranged signal, making certain "bunching" does not result.

2. Each opponent is marked closely and dribbler is denied any opportunity to move forward at conclusion of retreat.

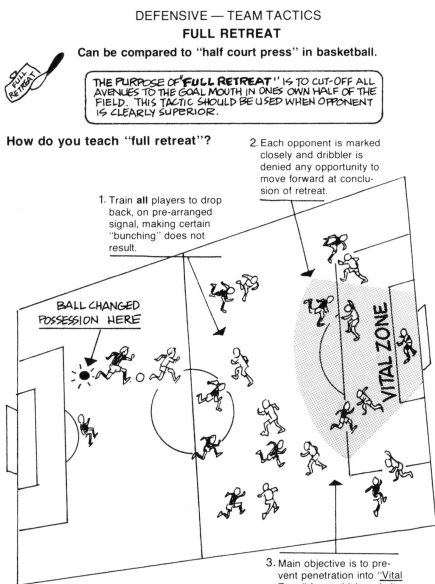

BALL CHANGED
POSSESSION HERE

VITAL ZONE

3. Main objective is to prevent penetration into "Vital Zone" from which majority of all goals are scored.

NOTE:
"**FULL RETREAT**" OFTEN RESULTS IN BUNCHING UP --
TO PREVENT BUNCHING UP, PLAYERS SHOULD BE TAUGHT
"FUNNELLING".

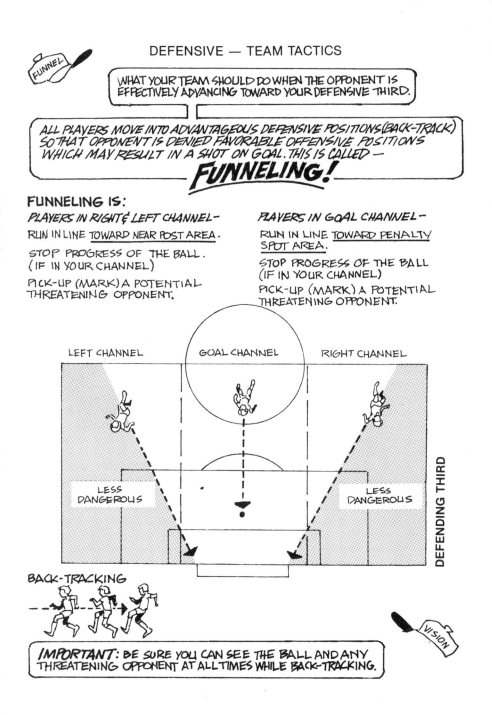

DEFENSIVE — TEAM TACTICS

FUNNEL

WHAT YOUR TEAM SHOULD DO WHEN THE OPPONENT IS EFFECTIVELY ADVANCING TOWARD YOUR DEFENSIVE THIRD.

ALL PLAYERS MOVE INTO ADVANTAGEOUS DEFENSIVE POSITIONS (BACK-TRACK) SO THAT OPPONENT IS DENIED FAVORABLE OFFENSIVE POSITIONS WHICH MAY RESULT IN A SHOT ON GOAL. THIS IS CALLED —

FUNNELING!

FUNNELING IS:

PLAYERS IN RIGHT & LEFT CHANNEL —

RUN IN LINE TOWARD NEAR POST AREA.

STOP PROGRESS OF THE BALL. (IF IN YOUR CHANNEL)

PICK-UP (MARK) A POTENTIAL THREATENING OPPONENT.

PLAYERS IN GOAL CHANNEL —

RUN IN LINE TOWARD PENALTY SPOT AREA.

STOP PROGRESS OF THE BALL (IF IN YOUR CHANNEL)

PICK-UP (MARK) A POTENTIAL THREATENING OPPONENT.

LEFT CHANNEL   GOAL CHANNEL   RIGHT CHANNEL

LESS DANGEROUS

LESS DANGEROUS

DEFENDING THIRD

BACK-TRACKING

VISION

IMPORTANT: BE SURE YOU CAN SEE THE BALL AND ANY THREATENING OPPONENT AT ALL TIMES WHILE BACK-TRACKING.

SUMMERIZED. IT IS ESSENTIAL THAT YOUNG PLAYERS BE TAUGHT HOW THE FORWARD PLAYERS, MID-FIELD PLAYERS AND BACK PLAYERS WORK AS A UNIT OR **"TEAM"**. RATHER THAN HAVE BACKS STAND ON THE PENALTY AREA LINE, LIKE GUARDS ON DUTY, ALL PLAYERS REGARDLESS OF POSITION SHOULD BE TAUGHT TO MOVE WITH THE EBB AND FLOW OF THE GAME. THIS **MAY** MEAN **BACKS** MOVING UP TO THE FRONT LINE AS THE GAME SITUATION ALLOWS.

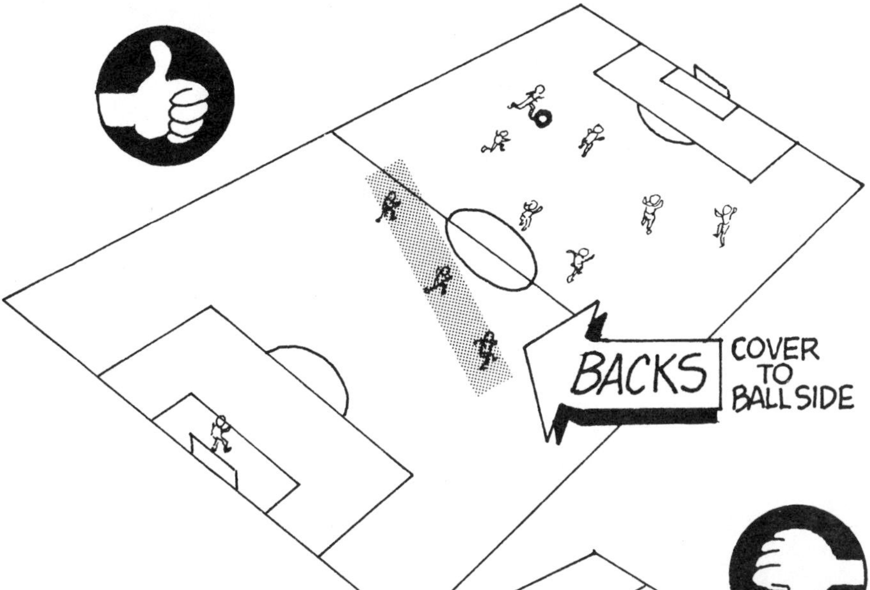

BACKS COVER TO BALL SIDE

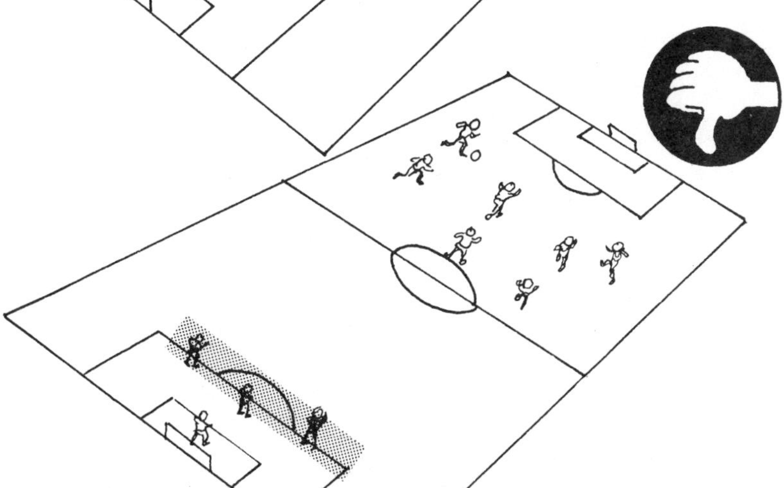

117

DEFENSIVE — TEAM TACTICS
TEAM VOCABULARY:

ONLY BY CONSTANT PRACTICE CAN TEAM MEMBERS "*TALK*" TO EACH OTHER DURING THE GAME "*TALKING*" INCLUDES WORDS, SIGNALS AND BODY LANGUAGE.

HERE ARE SOME EXAMPLES:

VERBAL

I'VE GOT #10 WHO HAS #3?

SIGNAL
WAVING ARM IN A CERTAIN DIRECTION.

BODY LANGUAGE
"DEFENSIVE STANCE" TO ENCOURAGE BALL RIGHT OR LEFT.

There are no rules for how information is to be given.
IF IT WORKS — THEN IT IS RIGHT!

118

LAWS of the GAME
for Under 6 Players.

MODIFIED LAWS
UNDER-6 PLAYERS

LAW 1. FIELD OF PLAY.

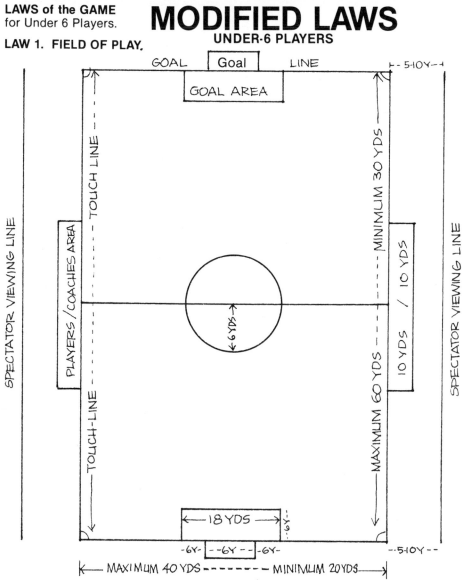

A. DIMENSIONS:
The field of play shall be rectangular. The length shall exceed the width. (See Diagram)

B. MARKINGS:
Distinctive lines from 2-5 inches wide, Halfway line, Center circle, Four corner arcs, Goal area, Players/Coaches Area, Spectator Viewing Line. (See Diagram).

C. THE GOALS:
The goals shall consist of two upright posts six yards apart and equidistant from the corner flags.
Measurements: Six feet high and
                 Six yards wide. (Eighteen feet wide).

119

LAW 2. THE BALL
Size Three (#3)

LAW 3. NUMBER OF PLAYERS
- Five – No Goalkeeper.
- The maximum number of players on the roster should not exceed nine.
- Playing Time: Each player must participate a minimum of 50% of the total playing time.
- Substitution: During "substitution break" or at half time.
- Recommendation: Teams should be co-ed.

LAW 4. PLAYERS EQUIPMENT
- Jersey or shirt with number on back, shorts, stockings, footwear.

Note: A player shall not wear anything which is dangerous to another player or to himself.

LAW 5. REFEREE
- Shall be encouraged to explain an infraction to the offending player, without undue delay of the game or showing favoritism to either team. Referee should address both teams not an individual while doing so.
- If player continues to use incorrect skill after being advised by referee as to the correct method – allow play to continue but advise by word that error is being overlooked for the good of the game.

LAW 6. LINESMAN
Assist center referee on off-side, ball out of play and follow any instructions given by center referee.

LAW 7. DURATION OF THE GAME
- The game is to be divided into two halves of 15 minutes each.
- The "substitution break" shall be whistled by the referee mid-way through each half.
- Half-time break shall not exceed five minutes.

LAW 8. THE START OF PLAY
- Opponent must be 6 yards from the center mark when kick-off is being taken.

NOTE: The ball is not in play until it travels its own circumference and cannot be touched by kicker a second time until touched by another player.

LAW 9. BALL IN AND OUT PLAY
NOTE: The ball is out of play when it has wholly crossed the goal or touch lines.

LAW 10. METHOD OF SCORING
- The whole of the ball must cross the goal line between the goal posts and under the cross bar.
- The ball cannot be thrown, carried or intentionally propelled by hand or arm over the goal line.

LAW 11. OFF-SIDE
Conform to FIFA laws of the game

LAW 12. FOULS AND MISCONDUCT
- A "foul" is <u>any</u> play which possibly could result in injury.
- The referee should explain all infractions to the offending player in "less than 50" words.

Note: If explanation requires more than "50 words" wait for end of game to do so.

LAW 13. FREE KICKS
Shall be classified under ONE heading — "INDIRECT". This means — a goal may not be scored until the ball has been played or touched by a second player — of either team.

LAW 14. PENALTY KICKS
NO penalty kicks

LAW 15. THROW-IN
One rethrow must be allowed if foul throw occurs.
Referee shall explain fault before rethrow.

LAW 16. GOAL KICK
- Goal kick may be taken from any point inside the goal area – six yard area.
- Opponents must be six yards away from the ball.

LAW 17. CORNER KICK
- May be taken from any point inside the corner arcs.
- Opponents must be six yards away from the ball.

LAW 18. COMMON SENSE
- Do not make rules which will result in boredom, bureaucracy and losing sight of your purpose as an adult.
- Keep no league standings: No publicity.
- <u>Let them have FUN</u>.

MODIFIED LAWS

LAW 1. FIELD OF PLAY   **UNDER-8 PLAYERS**

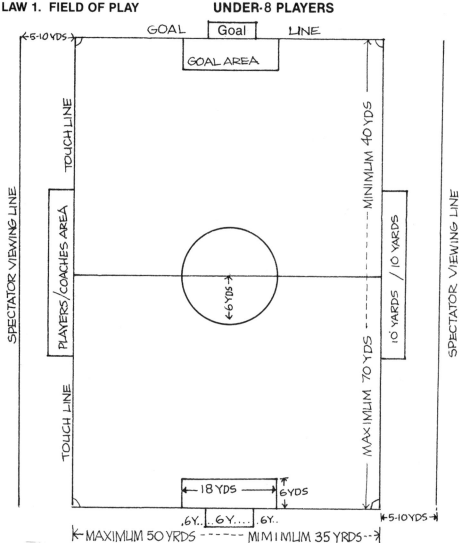

A. DIMENSIONS:
The field of play shall be rectangular. The length shall exceed the width. (See Diagram)

B. MARKINGS:
Distinctive lines from 2-5 inches wide, Halfway line, Center circle, Four corner arcs, Goal area, Players/Coaches Area, Spectator Viewing Line. (See Diagram).

C. THE GOALS:
The goals shall consist of two upright posts six yards apart and equidistant from the corner flags.
Measurements: Six feet high and
                Six yards wide. (Eighteen feet wide).

LAW 2. THE BALL
Size Three (#3)

LAW 3. NUMBER OF PLAYERS
• Seven – One of whom shall be a goalkeeper.

• The maximum number of players on the roster should not exceed eleven.

• Playing Time: Each player must participate a minimum of 50% of the total playing time.

• Substitution: During "substitution break" or at half time.

Recommendation: Teams should be co-ed.

LAW 4. PLAYERS EQUIPMENT
• Jersey or shirt with number on back, shorts, stockings, footwear.

Note: A player shall not wear anything which is dangerous to another player or to himself.

LAW 5. REFEREE
• Shall be encouraged to explain an infraction to the offending player, without undue delay of the game or showing favoritism to either team. Referee should address both teams not an individual while doing so.

• If player continues to use incorrect skill after being advised by referee as to the correct method – allow play to continue but advise by word error is being overlooked for the good of the game.

LAW 6. LINESMAN
Assist center referee on off-side and ball out of play and follow any instructions given by center referee.

LAW 7. DURATION OF THE GAME
• The game is to be divided into two halves of 20 minutes each.

• The "substitution break" shall be whistled by the referee mid-way through each half.

• Half-time break shall not exceed five minutes.

LAW 8. THE START OF PLAY
• Opponent must be 6 yards from the center mark when kick-off is being taken.

NOTE: The ball is not in play until it travels it's own circumference and cannot be touched by kicker a second time until touched by another player.

LAW 9. BALL IN AND OUT PLAY
NOTE: The ball is out of play when it has wholly crossed the goal or touch lines.

LAW 10. METHOD OF SCORING
• The whole of the ball must cross the goal line between the goal posts and under the cross bar.

• The ball cannot be thrown, carried or intentionally propelled by hand or arm over the goal line.

LAW 11. OFF-SIDE
Conform to FIFA laws of the game

LAW 12. FOULS AND MISCONDUCT
• A "foul" is <u>any</u> play which possibly could result in injury.

• The referee should explain all infractions to the offending player in "less than 50" words.
Note: If explanation requires more than "50 words", wait for end of game to do so.

LAW 13. FREE KICKS
Shall be classified under ONE heading – "INDIRECT".
This means – a goal may not be scored until the ball has been played or touched by a second player – of either team.

LAW 14. PENALTY KICKS
NO penalty kicks

LAW 15. THROW-IN
• One rethrow must be allowed if foul throw occurs.

• Referee shall explain fault before rethrow.

LAW 16. GOAL KICK
• Goal kick may be taken from any point inside the goal area – six yard area.

• Opponents must be six yards away from the ball.

LAW 17. CORNER KICK
• May be taken from any point inside the corner arcs.

• Opponents must be six yards away from the ball.

LAW 18. COMMON SENSE
• Do not make rules which will result in boredom, bureaucracy and losing sight of your purpose as an adult.

• Keep no league standings: No publicity.

• Let them have FUN.

MODIFIED LAWS

LAW 1. FIELD OF PLAY

UNDER-10 PLAYERS

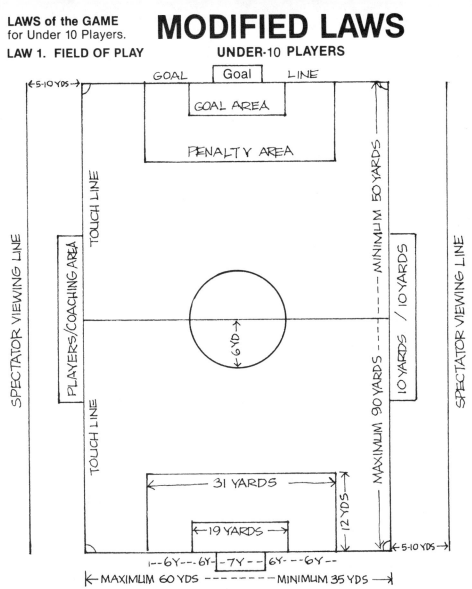

A. DIMENSIONS:
The field of play shall be rectangular. The length shall exceed the width. (See Diagram)

B. MARKINGS:
Distinctive lines from 2-5 inches wide, Halfway line, Center circle, Four corner arcs, Goal area, Penalty area, Players/Coaches Area, Spectator Viewing Line. (See Diagram).

C. THE GOALS:
The goals shall consist of two upright posts six yards apart and equidistant from the corner flags.
Measurements: Seven feet high and
                Seven yards wide. (Twenty one feet wide).

LAW 2.   THE BALL
Size Four (#4)

LAW 3.   NUMBER OF PLAYERS
•Nine – One of whom shall be a goalkeeper.

•The maximum number of players on the roster should not exceed thirteen.

•Playing Time: Each player must participate a minimum of 50% of the total playing time.

•Substitution: During any normal stoppage of the game

Recommendation: Teams should be co-ed.

LAW 4.   PLAYERS EQUIPMENT
•Jersey or shirt with number on back, shorts, stockings, footwear.

Note: A player shall not wear anything which is dangerous to another player or to himself.

LAW 5.   REFEREE
•Shall be encouraged to explain an infraction to the offending player, without undue delay of the game or showing favoritism to either team. Referee should address both teams not an individual while doing so.

•If player continues to use incorrect skill after being advised by referee as to the correct method – allow play to continue but advise by word error is being overlooked for the good of the game.

LAW 6.   LINESMAN
Assist center referee on off-side and ball out of play and follow any instructions given by center referee.

LAW 7.   DURATION OF THE GAME
•The game is to be divided into two halves of 25 minutes each.

•Half-time break shall not exceed five minutes.

LAW 8.   THE START OF PLAY
•Opponent must be 6 yards from the center mark when kick-off is being taken.

NOTE: The ball is not in play until it travels it's own circumference and cannot be touched by kicker a second time until touched by another player.

LAW 9.   BALL IN AND OUT PLAY
NOTE: The ball is out of play when it has wholly crossed the goal or touch lines.

LAW 10.   METHOD OF SCORING
•The whole of the ball must cross the goal line between the goal posts and under the cross bar.

•The ball cannot be thrown, carried or intentionally propelled by hand or arm over the goal line.

LAW 11. OFF-SIDE
Conform to FIFA laws of the game

LAW 12. FOULS AND MISCONDUCT
•Resulting in DIRECT FREE KICK:
•Fouls by hand:
Handling the ball. Holding, Pushing, Striking the opponent (Intentionally).
•Fouls by feet:
Tripping, Kicking and Jumping at the opponent (Intentionally).
•Fouls by body:
Charging from Behind, Violent Charging. (Intentionally).
All other fouls result in INDIRECT FREE KICK.

LAW 13. FREE KICKS
•DIRECT FREE KICK – A goal can be scored direct against the opponent from the point of infraction.
•INDIRECT FREE KICK – A goal may be scored against the opposing team only if the ball is touched by a second player of either team.

LAW 14. PENALTY KICKS
NO penalty kicks.

LAW 15. THROW-IN
•One rethrow must be allowed if foul throw occurs.
Referee shall explain fault before rethrow.

LAW 16. GOAL KICK
• Goal kick may be taken from any point inside the goal area – six yard area.
Opponents must be outside of penalty area.

LAW 17. CORNER KICK
•May be taken from any point inside the corner arcs.
Opponents must be six yards away from the ball.

LAW 18. COMMON SENSE
•Do not make rules which will result in boredom, bureaucracy and losing sight of your purpose as an adult
•Keep no league standings: No publicity.
•Let them have FUN.